U.S. OWNERSHIP OF FIRMS IN CANADA: ISSUES AND POLICY APPROACHES

Steven Globerman
York University

CANADA-U.S. PROSPECTS
a series sponsored by
C. D. Howe Research Institute (Canada)
National Planning Association (U.S.A.)

Legal Deposit — 2nd Quarter 1979
Quebec National Library
Library of Congress Catalog Number 79-51649
ISBN 0-88806-052-1
May, 1979, $5.00
Quotation with appropriate credit is permissible
C. D. Howe Research Institute (Montreal, Quebec) and
National Planning Association (Washington, D.C.)
Printed in Canada

CONTENTS

		Page
THE CANADA-U.S. PROSPECTS SERIES AND ITS SPONSORING ORGANIZATIONS		Inside front and back covers
FOREWORD		vi
ACKNOWLEDGMENTS		vii
I	CANADIAN-U.S. ECONOMIC LINKAGES THROUGH THE DIRECT INVESTMENT PROCESS	1
	1 Introduction	3
	2 Direct Investment in the Postwar Period	6
	Book Values	6
	Sectoral Distributions.................................	10
	3 Determinants of Foreign Direct and Portfolio Investment	14
	A Model of the Direct Investment Process	16
	Cost of Transferring Technology and Marketing Expertise .	16
	Summary	22
	4 Empirical Analysis of U.S. Foreign Direct Investment	23
	Changes in the Geographical Distribution of U.S. Foreign Direct Investment	23
	Cross-Section Industry Studies of U.S. Direct Investment in Canada	24
	Some Additional Cross-Section Evidence	26
	Technical Appendix A: An Analysis of the Geographical Distribution of U.S. Foreign Direct Investment	29
	5 Impact of Foreign Direct Investment on the Host Country	34
	Some Empirical Estimates	35
	Productivity of Foreign Direct Investment	37
	Impact of Foreign Direct Investment on Domestic Savings	39
	Indirect Effects of Foreign Direct Investment	40
	Recapitulation	42
	6 Bilateral Direct Investment: A Policy Overview	43

7 Conclusion 46

**Technical Appendix B: Determinants of Exporting Versus
   Subsidiary Selling in U.S. Companies** 48

**Technical Appendix C: An Empirical Analysis of
   Indirect Productivity Benefits** 51

Tables

1 Foreign Direct Investment in Canada, Selected Years,
   1945-74 7
2 Canadian Direct Investment Abroad, Selected Years,
   1945-74 7
3 Foreign Direct Investment in the United States, 1950,
   1965, and 1974 8
4 U.S. Foreign Direct Investment Abroad, 1950, 1966, and
   1974 8
5 Canadian Private Long-Term Investment Abroad, 1945,
   1964, and 1974 9
6 U.S. Private Long-Term Investment Abroad, 1945, 1966,
   and 1974 9
7 Foreign Direct Investment, by Sector, in Canada and the
   United States, 1974 9
8 Non-Resident Majority Ownership in the Canadian
   Manufacturing Industry, 1968 and 1973 11
9 U.S. Direct Investment, Selected Manufacturing
   Industries, 1973 12

**II CANADA'S FOREIGN INVESTMENT REVIEW ACT:
   AN ECONOMIC APPRAISAL** 55

1 Introduction 57

2 Background to the Act 62

**3 A General Framework for Evaluating FIRA's Economic
   Effects** 65
   Imperfectly Competitive Markets and Takeover "Rents" 65
   Power in Product Markets 66
   Efficiency Motives 72

4 An Overview of the Basic Issues 74

FIRA's Potential Direct and Indirect Effects on Aggregate
  Income 75
Potential Redistribution Effects 80

**5 Evidence Regarding FIRA's Effects on Foreign
    Acquisitions** 82

6 The Canadian Appliance Industry: A Case Study 86
A Brief History of the Case 87
Efficiency Considerations 89

7 Summary and Conclusions 95

Tables

1 Summary of FIRA Reviewable Acquisition Cases and
     Percentage of Resolved Cases Allowed, April 9,
     1974-December 30, 1977 58
2 Summary of FIRA Reviewable New-Business Cases and
     Percentage of Resolved Cases Allowed, October 15,
     1975-December 30, 1977 58
3 Average Assets of Acquirees, 1974/75-76/77 59
4 Reviewable Acquisition Cases, by Industry Sector,
     1974/75-76/77 59
5 Reviewable Acquisition Cases, 1974/75-76/77 71
6 Domestic and Foreign Control of Establishments
     Manufacturing Major Appliances, 1972 90
7 Estimates of Optimal Scale 91
8 Long-Run Unit Costs As Percentages of Optimum at
     Different Output Levels 91
9 Manufactures of Major Appliances, 1974 91

FOREWORD

The term foreign direct investment refers to international capital flows that result in outside ownership control over a country's production facilities. On a per capita basis, Canadians have made more direct investments in the United States than Americans have in Canada. Because of the vast disparity in the overall size of the two economies, however, total U.S. direct investment has reached such a high level in Canada that it is a topic of considerable controversy in the bilateral relationship. This two-part volume focuses upon the economic dimensions of this controversy.

In the first part of this volume, many of the issues that have been raised about U.S. direct investment in Canada are analyzed in order to examine how, and with what consequences, such investment affects the degree to which the two economies have become linked. The second part contains a review and analysis of Canada's recent steps to control foreign-direct-investment inflows through the Foreign Investment Review Agency (FIRA). This part of the volume is one of several case studies dealing with the bilateral consequences of various government policy actions that have been prepared for the Canada-U.S. Prospects series.

The author of this volume, Steven Globerman, is an Associate Professor in the Faculty of Administrative Studies at York University in Ontario. His approach is based on a comprehensive survey of the literature on direct investment and on statistical analyses that he undertook as part of this project. The conclusions he reaches suggest that the economic contribution of foreign direct investment to the host country tends to be understated in much of the commentary on this issue. He further suggests that the costs associated with FIRA may be borne primarily by Canadians.

Professor Globerman is guarded about the conclusions he reaches. The issues he has addressed are complex, and the data he was forced to work with are inadequate to allow definitive results, but he has attempted to provide a professional assessment of a topic that has been the subject of a good deal of emotion-based commentary in the past.

Barriers to foreign direct investment give rise to certain economic costs. Many Canadians, however, believe that foreign direct investment also gives rise to costs, both economic and non-economic, that require the imposition of some restraints. The purpose of this volume is not to advocate a particular policy approach but to contribute to a better understanding of the potential sacrifices involved in limitations on this form of capital movement. Other views and commentary on this issue are contained in companion volumes prepared for the Canada-U.S. Prospects series.

Carl E. Beigie
Series Coordinator

ACKNOWLEDGMENTS

The author thanks Professors Don Daly, Joseph McGuire, Edward Safarian, and Tom Wilson and Carl Beigie of the C. D. Howe Research Institute for helpful comments on earlier drafts of the first study in this volume and Professors Charles McMillan and Bernard Wolf for their extensive comments on earlier versions of the second study. Useful criticism of the FIRA study was also provided by Carl Beigie and by participants in seminar workshops held at the University of Toronto and at York University, where an earlier draft of the monograph was discussed. Mr. G. H. Dewhirst, Director of the Research and Analysis Branch of the Foreign Investment Review Agency, kindly provided an unsolicited working paper by Louis Calvet, which was of particular benefit in producing the final version of the study on FIRA. In spite of the extensive inputs provided by outside readers, there are, no doubt, residual shortcomings in the volume. Any remaining errors or other weaknesses of the volume are the sole responsibility of the author.

I

CANADIAN-U.S. ECONOMIC LINKAGES THROUGH THE DIRECT INVESTMENT PROCESS

1

Introduction

The balance of advantages and disadvantages of closer economic integration with the United States is an issue of long-standing importance and controversy among Canadians. In recent years particular attention has been focused upon U.S. foreign direct investment in Canada as a major feature of the integration that exists. Canadian concern about the effects of unrestricted direct investment capital inflows was manifested in federal legislation establishing the Foreign Investment Review Agency (FIRA) in 1974. While the rate of growth of such investment in Canada has slowed over the past decade, and even though FIRA has been put in place to "deal with" certain types of foreign investment, U.S. direct investment will likely remain an important policy issue in Canada. Absolute increases in the book value of foreign direct investment will remain substantial even if the rate of growth continues to decline.

An acceleration of foreign direct investment in the United States over the past few years has led to a heightened awareness among Washington officials of host-country concerns about foreign direct investment.[1] Furthermore, the effects on the domestic economy of direct investment abroad continue to be an important concern of the U.S. labor movement as well as a subject of public policy debate.[2] Recent and proposed changes to tax legislation affecting the foreign subsidiaries of U.S. companies may generate an intensified debate about the net benefits of foreign direct investment to both host and home countries.[3]

---

[1] In 1974 the U.S. Congress established a mandate under the Foreign Investment Study Act to investigate growing foreign investment in the United States.

[2] Recent political developments in this debate are reviewed in Richard Barovick, "The Washington Struggle over Multinationals," *Business and Society Review*, No. 18, Summer, 1976, pp. 12-19. It is noteworthy that outbound foreign direct investment appears to be emerging as an important policy issue in Canada as well. More specifically, certain Canadian labor groups have recently expressed a concern about the export of capital from Canada (see Wilfrid List, "Investment Abroad Hurts Jobs, Meeting Told," *Globe and Mail* [Toronto], February 2, 1978).

[3] One recent change in U.S. tax law was the implementation of new guidelines for sections 861 to 864 of the Internal Revenue Code, which create an incentive for U.S. investors to charge their foreign subsidiaries more for research and development

3

Against the projected background of continued interest in the magnitude and the effects of bilateral direct investment, a re-examination of the phenomenon of foreign ownership seems appropriate. While a substantial literature has been developed on the subject of international production, significant confusion and disagreement continue to exist on such fundamental issues as the underlying causes of foreign direct investment and the costs and benefits of foreign ownership to the host and home countries of multinational corporations.[4] Thus a successful clarification of the ambiguities related to the causes and effects of foreign ownership could make an important contribution to resolving ongoing policy debates.

This paper attempts to place into perspective several important concerns related to the bilateral foreign direct investment process. In particular, it considers two broad issues of potential relevance to policies affecting bilateral direct investment flows. One is the extent to which direct investment and long-term portfolio investment are equivalent means of transferring capital between countries. The other is the economic implication (for both host and home countries) of increased or decreased foreign direct investment. Obviously, the issues chosen do not encompass all the considerations relevant in evaluating the direct investment process. Indeed, no contribution of modest length could provide a comprehensive treatment of even the two issues cited above. Nevertheless, the substitutability among forms of capital investment determines the ultimate effects of attempting to exchange one form of foreign investment for another. Furthermore, any effort to evaluate the economic impact of foreign investment that overlooks potential differences between direct and indirect investment runs a serious risk of reaching erroneous conclusions. Thus the issues considered in this monograph are of inescapable importance to policy-makers.

The major theme of this monograph is that foreign direct investment and foreign indirect investment are imperfect substitutes. The degree of substitutability varies across different industries according to the types of products produced and the characteristics of firms in the industries. Thus the economic impact of obstacles to bilateral direct investment will not be exactly offset by changes in foreign portfolio investment. This argument, which is not unduly contentious in and of itself, can be shown to have significant

---

undertaken by the parent company. Other changes that may be implemented include elimination of the deferral of U.S. taxes on foreign subsidiaries' retained earnings and repeal of the foreign tax credit. The potential impact of such changes upon U.S. capital flows abroad is considered in Thomas Horst, "American Taxation of Multinational Firms," *American Economic Review* 67, No. 3 (June, 1977):376-90.

[4] An appreciation of the inconclusive nature of existing studies surrounding these issues can be gained from surveys of the literature provided in Government of Canada, *Foreign Direct Investment in Canada* (Ottawa, 1972), and in John H. Dunning, "The Determinants of International Production," *Oxford Economic Papers* 25, No. 3 (November, 1973): 289-336.

implications for estimates of the net economic benefits of foreign direct investment. Specifically, estimates of the economic impact of foreign direct investment that treat such investment as being equivalent to any other form of capital inflow are likely to understate the net economic benefits of foreign direct investment for the host economy.[5] By focusing on specific studies of the economic contribution of foreign investment in Canada, this monograph identifies the specific sources of bias that result from a failure to acknowledge differences between foreign direct investment and other forms of investment. More specifically, a case is made that existing studies probably underestimate the net economic benefits of foreign direct investment, particularly for the host country.

The analysis relies heavily upon a synthesis of the relevant literature; some original empirical work bearing upon important hypotheses is also discussed. No attempt is made to provide comprehensive answers to the questions addressed. The aim of this study is, instead, to contribute to a better understanding of the causes and consequences of direct investment and, in turn, to a fuller appreciation of the potential impact of legislation upon the direct investment process.

Before considering the issues identified above, a brief overview of the postwar bilateral direct investment process is presented.[6] This overview provides a quantitative perspective on bilateral direct investment and supplies some empirical evidence relevant to testing hypotheses regarding its causes and effects.

---

[5] In this context, economic impact can be defined as the average rate of return to capital.

[6] An excellent historical review of prewar direct investment in Canada is provided in Hugh G. J. Aitken, *American Capital and Canadian Resources* (Cambridge, Mass.: Harvard University Press, 1961). A consideration of bilateral capital flows over the period 1950-63 is offered in Irving Brecher, *Capital Flows Between Canada and the United States* (Montreal: Private Planning Association of Canada, 1965).

2

Direct Investment in the Postwar Period

The essential distinction between direct investment and portfolio investment is that the former involves legal control of the underlying real asset. Foreign direct investment is largely represented by equity capital in the form of shares of incorporated subsidiaries and net assets of unincorporated branches plus loans from parents to subsidiaries and affiliates. Portfolio investment covers purchases of public issues of bonds and debentures of corporations and governments as well as minority holdings of securities. In the Canadian experience, foreign portfolio investment has been mainly in government and corporate bonds and debentures.[1]

Book Values

Tables 1 and 2 report book values of foreign direct investment in Canada and of Canadian direct investment abroad for selected years. The value of foreign direct investment in Canada includes the reinvested earnings of foreign subsidiaries. Until about 1963, net capital inflows of direct investment exceeded the net increase in undistributed earnings of Canadian subsidiaries; since 1963 this relationship has been reversed. The value of Canadian direct investment abroad includes investments by foreign-owned enterprises in Canada. Approximately 65 percent of Canadian direct investment abroad in 1970 was controlled by Canadian residents.[2]

Data in Tables 1 and 2, reveal that, in absolute dollar terms, the United States is the largest direct investor in Canada as well as the main recipient of Canadian foreign direct investment; however, the relative importance of the United States to Canada's direct investment position (as both recipient and investor) has decreased over the postwar period. Specifically, the value of U.S. direct investment in Canada as a ratio of all foreign direct investment in Canada declined from .85 in 1945 to .80 in 1974. The bulk of the decline took

---

[1] The distinction between direct and portfolio investment is taken from A. E. Safarian, *Foreign Ownership of Canadian Industry* (Toronto: McGraw-Hill, 1966).
[2] These data are from Statistics Canada, *Canada's International Investment Position* (Ottawa, 1977).

TABLE 1

Foreign Direct Investment in Canada, Selected Years, 1945-74
(million Canadian dollars)

	1945	1950	1955	1961	1967	1971	1974
United States	2,304	3,426	6,513	11,284	17,000	22,443	28,996
United Kingdom	348	468	890	1,613	2,152	2,715	3,525
Other countries	61	81	325	840	1,547	2,760	3,716
	2,713	3,975	7,728	13,727	20,699	27,918	36,237

Sources: Statistics Canada, *The Canadian Balance of International Payments* (Ottawa, various issues) and *Canada's International Investment Position*, 1974 (Ottawa, 1978).

TABLE 2

Canadian Direct Investment Abroad, Selected Years, 1945-74
(million Canadian dollars)

	1945	1949	1954	1960	1968	1971	1974
United States	455	721	1,231	1,618	2,546	3,388	4,909
United Kingdom	54	59	119	257	570	590	879
Other countries	211	146	269	592	1,501	2,556	3,519
	720	926	1,619	2,467	4,617	6,534	9,307

Sources: See Table 1.

place after 1955. The value of Canadian direct investment in the United States as a ratio of total Canadian direct investment abroad declined from .63 in 1945 to .53 in 1974. Since the ratio actually reached a peak value in the mid-1950s, its decline set in toward the latter part of the 1950s. It is interesting to note that, while the value of foreign direct investment in Canada increased at a faster rate than the value of Canadian direct investment abroad over the entire sample period, the converse has been true in recent years.

Tables 3 and 4 report data for foreign direct investment for the United States that support the notion that bilateral direct investment became relatively less important over the postwar period. The ratio of U.S. foreign direct investment in Canada to total U.S. foreign direct investment remained at approximately .30 over the period 1950-66, after which it declined to around .24 in 1974. The value of Canadian foreign direct investment in the United States as a ratio of total foreign direct investment in the United States declined continuously over the sample period, from .30 to .22. Over the latter half of the postward period, EEC countries became an increasingly important recipient of U.S. foreign direct investment as well as a more prominent source of direct investment in the United States.

TABLE 3

Foreign Direct Investment in the United States, 1950, 1965, and 1974
(million U.S. dollars)

	1950	1965	1974
Canada	1,029	2,388	4,806
United Kingdom	1,168	2,852	6,126
Other European countries	1,059	3,224	7,973
Other countries	135	333	2,842
	3,391	8,797	21,747

Source: U.S. Department of Commerce, *Survey of Current Business* (Washington, D.C.: U.S. Government Printing Office, various issues).

TABLE 4

U.S. Foreign Direct Investment Abroad, 1950, 1966, and 1974
(million U.S. dollars)

	1950	1966	1974
Canada	3,579	15,713	28,378
Europe	1,733	16,390	44,505
Other countries	6,476	19,689	45,729
	11,788	51,792	118,613

Source: See Table 3.

The relative importance of direct investment compared to other forms of bilateral private long-term foreign investment is indicated in the data in Tables 5 and 6. Quite clearly, the bulk of private bilateral long-term foreign investment over the postwar period has taken the form of direct investment. It is suggestive that direct investment is the predominant vehicle for the transfer of private capital abroad for both Canada and the United States.[3] Furthermore, this predominance is evident not only for bilateral transfers but also for Canadian and U.S. transfers to third countries. It would seem that direct investment has afforded important advantages, on average, to both Canadian and U.S. exporters of private capital. The precise nature of these advantages is relevant to a determination of the net economic effects of foreign ownership, and a later section of this paper will explore in some detail potential reasons for the preponderance of transfers of private capital in the form of direct investment.

[3] The implications of this observation for a theory of foreign direct investment will be considered in more detail later in the study.

TABLE 5

Canadian Private Long-Term Investment Abroad, 1945, 1964, and 1974
(million Canadian dollars)

	United States			All Countries		
	1945	1964	1974	1945	1964	1974
Direct investment	455	2,025	4,909	720	3,356	9,307
Portfolio holdings	409	1,445	2,967	621	1,932	3,924
	864	3,470	8,476	1,341	5,288	18,818

Sources: See Table 1.

TABLE 6

U.S. Private Long-Term Investment Abroad, 1945, 1966, and 1974
(million U.S. dollars)

	Canada			All Countries		
	1945	1966	1974	1945	1966	1974
Direct investment	2,907	16,999	28,404	8,370	54,777	118,600
Portfolio investment	2,858	9,566	15,906	3,827	21,004	41,400
	5,765	26,565	44,310	12,197	75,781	16,000

Source: See Table 3.

TABLE 7

**Foreign Direct Investment, by Sector, in Canada and
the United States, 1974**

Sector	Canada (mil. Can. $)	United States (mil. U.S. $)
Manufacturing	14,796	10,685
Petroleum/gas	8,934	5,979
Mining/smelting	4,032	n.a.s.
Merchandising	2,375	n.a.s.
Financial/insurance	4,309	2,864
Other	1,791	2,893
	36,237	22,421

n.a.s. = not available separately
Sources: Statistics Canada, *Canada's International Investment Position, op. cit.*; and
U.S. Department of Commerce, *op. cit.*

Sectoral Distributions

A tentative insight into the nature of the direct investment process can be gained by considering the distribution, by industrial sector, of foreign direct investment. Table 7 reports 1974 book values of foreign direct investment, by major industrial sector, for Canada and the United States. It can be seen that in the United States the bulk of such investment is concentrated in the manufacturing and petroleum sectors. This concentration is particularly marked if one standardizes the sectoral value of direct investment by the total asset sizes of the various sectors in the U.S. economy.[4] The bulk of foreign direct investment in Canada is concentrated in the manufacturing, petroleum, and mining/smelting sectors. The percentage of total foreign direct investment in Canada comprising investment in manufacturing remained roughly constant over the postwar period, while the percentage of foreign direct investment in the petroleum sector increased somewhat.

While not shown separately, U.S. direct investment abroad has been directed to the petroleum and particularly the manufacturing sectors of recipient countries. Roughly 47 percent of U.S. direct investment in Canada is concentrated in the manufacturing sector, compared to 53 percent for Europe and 36 percent for all other countries. The distribution of U.S. direct investment in Canada and Europe across major sectors has remained roughly constant over the postwar period. In other countries there has been an increase in manufacturing direct investment relative to direct investment in the petroleum sector.[5] The bulk of Canadian direct investment abroad has been in the manufacturing and commercial sectors. A substantially smaller percentage of Canadian, as compared to U.S., foreign direct investment has been directed toward the petroleum sectors of foreign countries.

Substantial differences exist in the degree of foreign ownership across manufacturing industries. This point is illustrated for Canada in Table 8, which reports, for a sample of two-digit industries, the percentage of industry assets that were majority-owned by nonresidents in 1968 and 1973. Industries with relatively high foreign ownership levels include petroleum products, rubber products, transportation equipment, tobacco, and chemical products. Industries with relatively low percentages of foreign ownership include furniture,

---

[4] For example, in 1970 the ratio of manufacturing assets to total industrial assets in the United States was approximately .23; the book value of foreign direct investment in manufacturing as a ratio of the total book value of foreign direct investment was closer to .50. The respective ratios for the petroleum sector are approximately .01 and .22.

[5] The changing pattern of direct investment in third countries reflects, to some extent, the increasing emphasis of U.S. multinational firms on international subcontracting (see Michael Sharpston, "International Sub-Contracting," *Oxford Economic Papers* 27, No. 1 [March, 1975]:94-135).

TABLE 8

Non-Resident Majority Ownership^a in the Canadian
Manufacturing Industry, 1968 and 1973
(percentages)

Industry	1968	1973
Food and beverages	31.2	34.7
Tobacco	84.3	100.0
Rubber products	93.1	86.2
Leather products	22.0	28.1
Textile	39.4	68.5
Wood	30.7	13.4
Furniture	18.9	21.4
Printing, publishing, and allied	21.0	11.8
Paper and allied products	39.4	44.5
Primary metals	55.3	36.2
Metal fabricating	46.9	42.5
Machinery	71.8	70.9
Transport equipment	86.6	89.5
Electrical products	64.2	59.3
Non-metallic mineral products	51.5	67.3
Petroleum and coal products	99.5	97.2
Chemicals and chemical products	81.5	87.5
Miscellaneous manufacturing	53.9	55.2

^{a}As measured by assets.

Sources: Government of Canada, *Foreign Direct Investment in Canada* (Ottawa, 1972), Table 5, p. 21; Statistics Canada, *Calura Annual Report* (Ottawa, 1976).

leather, printing, wood, and food and beverages. Data for earlier and later years suggest that, while foreign ownership ratios have varied over time, the order of Canadian manufacturing industries ranked by the percentage of foreign ownership has remained relatively constant over the postwar period.

Some additional evidence on the sectoral specificity of foreign direct investment is provided in Table 9, which shows the value of U.S. direct investment in selected manufacturing industries for a sample of developed countries. The data indicate striking similarities in the allocation of U.S. direct investment across countries. For example, six countries, including Canada, report data separately for the five specific sample industries. We find that the machinery industry has the highest relative percentage of U.S. direct investment in five of the six countries, while the primary and fabricated metals sector has the lowest relative percentage in five of the six countries. Transportation equipment, followed by chemicals and food, is the most commonly observed order of relative investment intensity for the remaining sample industries in the various countries.

TABLE 9

U.S. Direct Investment, Selected Manufacturing Industries, 1973
(million U.S. dollars)

	All Manufacturing	Food	Chemicals and Allied	Primary and Fabricated Metals	Machinery	Transport Equipment	Other Manufacturing
Canada	11,755	1,102	1,767	779	2,325	2,249	3,532
United Kingdom	6,611	576	1,042	343	2,008	1,186	1,456
Belgium	1,497	62	467	72	518	n.s.s.	n.s.s.
France	2,946	186	453	119	1,011	481	693
Germany	4,449	244	578	291	1,683	1,299	345
Italy	1,413	130	350	73	586	101	149
Netherlands	1,204	120	402	148	267	n.s.s.	n.s.s.
Denmark	72	n.s.s.	12	5	n.s.s.	n.s.s.	n.s.s.
Spain	571	110	124	n.s.s.	165	n.s.s.	74
Sweden	429	n.s.s.	31	30	236	n.s.s.	103
Switzerland	702	68	73	53	100	n.s.s.	n.s.s.
Japan	1,399	n.s.s.	301	11	732	116	n.s.s.
Australia	2,025	195	498	102	363	483	384
South Africa	501	69	85	35	91	n.s.s.	n.s.s.

n.s.s. = not shown separately

Source: U.S. Department of Commerce, *Survey of Current Business*, October, 1975 (Washington, D.C.: U.S. Government Printing Office, 1976).

Since the values reported in Table 9 are not standardized for the overall sizes of the sample industries, the similarity in the industrial distribution of foreign ownership will, to some extent, simply reflect the similar size distribution of industries across the sample countries. Nevertheless, given a presumed potential for the importation of portfolio, as opposed to direct, investment capital, the similarities noted above provide some evidence that U.S. direct investment is a particularly preferred means of transferring capital to specific industries.

The important features of bilateral direct investment in the postwar period can be summarized as follows: The United States remains the major single source of foreign direct investment in Canada, although in recent years it has been a relatively less important source compared to some other countries. U.S. direct investment in third countries (particularly in Europe), relative to Canada, increased over the latter part of the postwar period. Similarly, while the United States remains the single largest repository for Canadian foreign direct investment, its relative importance has declined in recent years. The bulk of private long-term Canadian and U.S. foreign investment over the postwar period has taken the form of direct investment. The greatest percentage of Canadian and U.S. direct investment abroad is in manufacturing, while the bulk of foreign-owned assets in the two countries is held in the manufacturing and petroleum sectors. Within the manufacturing sector, foreign direct investment tends to be more prominent in some industries than in others.

3

Determinants of Foreign Direct and Portfolio Investment

Until the 1960s, foreign direct investment was generally considered to be just another (albeit important) form of international capital investment.[1] While the continued growth of multilateral direct investment in the postwar period has led to reconsideration of earlier theories and to a proliferation of alternative hypotheses, no clear understanding of the fundamental differences between direct investment and other forms of long-term capital investment has yet been in evidence in policy-related analyses of the process of foreign direct investment.

As an example of this confusion, the Gray Report admonishes against adopting simplistic notions about the need to import capital — including direct investment capital — to balance a current-account deficit during a period of expansion; however, the report goes on to suggest that anticipated surpluses in Canada's current account mean that foreign direct investment will be unnecessary to finance a current-account deficit in the balance of payments and that, even if Canada should in the future require a significant inflow of foreign capital to offset a current-account deficit, it should be possible to obtain that capital in forms other than that of direct investment.[2] As another example, a recent study by T. L. Powrie fails to make any distinction between foreign direct investment and foreign portfolio investment (or, indeed, between domestic savings and foreign savings) in evaluating the impact of foreign capital on Canada's economic growth.[3] Other observers of the foreign investment process, on the other hand, have emphasized that important differences exist between direct and portfolio investment (for example,

---

[1] See Giorgio Ragazzi, "Theories of the Determinants of Direct Foreign Investment," *International Monetary Fund Staff Papers* 20, No. 2 (July, 1973):471-97; and John H. Dunning, "The Determinants of International Production," *Oxford Economic Papers* 25, No. 3 (November, 1973):289-336.

[2] See Government of Canada, *Foreign Direct Investment in Canada* (Ottawa, 1972), pp. 82-84.

[3] T. L. Powrie, "The Contribution of Foreign Capital to Canadian Economic Growth," mimeographed, Department of Economics, University of Alberta, July, 1977.

direct investment usually involves a "package" of resources, and not just financial resources).[4] It would appear, therefore, that a clear and widely accepted set of distinctions among the various forms of foreign investment has yet to be drawn effectively in the policy literature.

The extent and the nature of any distinctions among various forms of foreign investment have, of course, important public-policy implications. For example, if portfolio investment and direct investment are, essentially, perfect substitutes, restrictions on inflows of foreign direct investment will have no impact upon the net inflow of private long-term capital, given any difference between expected real returns on domestic and foreign capital investment. Furthermore, perfect substitutability between direct and portfolio investment implies that the expected contributions of the two forms of capital importation to real economic growth are, on average, identical. That is, either form of net capital inflow enables a country to finance a deficit between its export earnings and its expenditures on imports; the capital-importing country thereby has more goods and services available to it, both because exports are smaller and because imports are larger than if the deficit could not be maintained. Alternatively, if portfolio investment and direct investment are imperfect substitutes, policies discouraging foreign direct investment (given any differential between expected domestic and foreign returns to capital) will reduce the net amount of foreign investment in a country.[5] In addition, if the growth-promoting impact of foreign direct investment differs from that associated with portfolio investment, the overall economic impact of a substitution of portfolio for direct investment will be non-neutral.

Even casual observation suggests that foreign direct investment and portfolio investment are not perfect substitutes. One obvious distinction is that direct investment is undertaken primarily by corporations, while individuals and institutional investors place funds abroad mainly in the form of securities.[6] Another is that direct investment often takes the form of an indivisible package of money, technology, skills, and markets.[7] Furthermore, direct investment tends to be concentrated in particular industries.[8] Such observations

---

[4] See, for example, Irving Brecher, *Capital Flows Between Canada and the United States* (Montreal: Private Planning Association of Canada, 1965); and Richard E. Caves, "International Corporations: The Industrial Economics of Foreign Investment," *Economica* 38 (February, 1971):18-44.

[5] The magnitude of the reduction will depend, in part, upon the elasticity of substitution between the two types of investment.

[6] Ragazzi, *op. cit.*, p. 477.

[7] This characteristic of foreign direct investment is cited in Brecher, *op. cit.*, p. 19, and in Caves, *op. cit.*

[8] This observation is also made in John McManus, "The Theory of the International Firm," in Gilles Paquet, ed., *The Multinational Firm and the Nation State* (Toronto: Ryerson Press, 1972).

suggest that potential differences exist between the determinants and the effects of foreign direct versus portfolio investment; however, the implications of the distinctions cited above can be better appreciated within the context of a model of the direct investment process. The outline of such a model has been developed by various authors, and our own effort takes the form primarily of integrating and synthesizing existing studies.

A Model of the Direct Investment Process

The starting point for any theory of international investment is the premise that international capital transfers will occur whenever anticipated risk-adjusted rates of return to capital differ among countries.[9] The expected return to invested capital in an activity will, in turn, depend upon the quantity of complementary inputs (for example, management, skilled labor, and technology) available for use in combination with capital. If complementary inputs can be transferred to the capital-importing sector more easily (or, equivalently, at lower cost) when they are part of an entire resource package (for example, in a direct investment transaction) than when they are parts of separate arm's-length transactions (for example, in the case of technology licensing financed by debt capital), the expected return to a direct investment capital transfer will exceed the expected return to a portfolio investment, other things being equal.[10] An essential feature of the direct investment process is that, along with an international transfer of capital, it involves the extension of managerial control. Therefore, the relative profitability of transferring capital through direct, rather than through portfolio, investment depends importantly upon the relationship between the efficiency with which productive resources are transferred between countries and the international scope of ownership in any given economic activity.[11]

Cost of Transferring Technology and Marketing Expertise

Existing studies of U.S. direct investment in Canadian manufacturing industries by and large concur that "intangible" assets associated with product differentiation and R & D performance primarily

---

[9] No attempt will be made here to consider the merits of alternative risk-adjusted return measures. It is merely noted that expected returns on any investment should net out transactions costs associated with transferring capital between countries. Furthermore, the riskiness of any investment should be evaluated as the investment's marginal contribution to the estimated risk of the firm's entire investment portfolio.

[10] It is important to bear in mind that this analysis considers resource transfers that will ordinarily continue over an extended period of time.

[11] Outlines of this argument can be found in the following: McManus, *op. cit.*; H. G. Baumann, "Merger Theory, Property Rights, and the Pattern of U.S. Direct Investment in Canada," *Weltwirtschafliches Archiv* 3, No. 4 (1975):677-98; and Peter J.

underlie whatever competitive advantages U.S. firms possess in Canadian markets.[12] Furthermore, it has been frequently noted that successful technology transfers often require a sustained relationship between transferors and transferees, such as that provided by the multinational-firm structure. This requirement is particularly relevant when the technological advantages of the foreign firm do not derive from some one-shot innovation in technique or product. Exporting and/or licensing will also be less preferred techniques for transferring technological resources when the technology-absorption capacity of recipients is relatively low and when the technology transferred is highly sophisticated and relatively new.[13] In short, costs associated with transferring technological resources are often minimized when the transfers are effected through intrafirm exchanges rather than by open market exchanges. In consequence, one might expect a higher average rate of return to direct investment, compared to portfolio investment, in those activities involving the ongoing transfer of sophisticated technological resources among potential users.

To elaborate upon the above argument, it is certainly possible for domestic entrepreneurs to attempt to borrow money abroad in order to purchase, or license, foreign technological resources for use in their home markets.[14] Domestic entrepreneurs would need to offer foreign lenders a rate of return at least equal to the rate of return the foreigners could expect to earn by investing directly in the entrepreneurs' domestic market.[15] However, if technological resources are transferred more efficiently through intracorporate than through intercorporate exchange, potential foreign lenders could expect to earn higher rates of return on direct investment than the rates of return that domestic entrepreneurs would pay for borrowed funds plus any royalty or licensing fees associated with the transfer of technological resources, other things being equal.[16] In effect, the

Buckley and Mark Casson, *The Future of the Multinational Enterprise* (London: Macmillan, 1976).

[12] See Thomas Horst, "The Industrial Composition of U.S. Exports and Subsidiary Sales to the Canadian Market," *American Economic Review* 62, No. 1 (March, 1972):37-46; Richard E. Caves, "Causes of Direct Investment: Foreign Firms' Shares in Canadian and United Kingdom Manufacturing Industries," *Review of Economics and Statistics* 56, No. 3 (August, 1974):279-93; and Baumann, *op. cit.*

[13] On these points, see Jack Baranson, "Technology Transfer Through the International Firm," *American Economic Review* 60, No. 2 (May, 1970):435-41. Recent empirical evidence on the determinants of technology transfer costs is provided in David Teece, "Technology Transfer by Multinational Firms: The Resource Cost of Transferring Technological Know-How," *Economic Journal* 87 (June, 1977):242-61.

[14] It is immaterial to our argument whether the borrowing and licensing activities are integrated or represent separate transactions. Another possibility, of course, is for domestic entrepreneurs to import new products developed abroad for resale in the domestic market. Such imports could, in turn, be financed by issuing debt or minority equity shares in domestic businesses.

[15] It is implicit that the relevant comparison is between risk-adjusted rates of return.

[16] A similar point is made in the following quote: "The design, production, sales and

increased efficiency associated with the international extension of managerial control over technological resources is reflected in a lower average cost of capital for direct as compared to portfolio investment. One would therefore expect impediments to incoming foreign direct investment to reduce overall foreign investment, particularly in technology-intensive industries.

It might be objected that a substantial number of successful transfers of technology through patent and know-how licenses can be identified. In particular, Japan is frequently pointed to as an example of how technology can be successfully attracted under licenses while avoiding foreign ownership. To some extent, the Japanese comparison is misleading since evidence suggests that, through much of the postwar period, the technology transferred may have been of a more standardized and less complex nature than was "best-practice" technology transferred from U.S. parent companies to their foreign affiliates.[17] Furthermore, transfers through the multinational corporation usually encompass associated managerial and marketing skills as well as technical information. Thus the typical "arm's-length" technology transfer to Japan is not identical to the typical transfer within U.S. subsidiaries. Specifically, technology transfers to Japan through much of the postwar period did not necessarily manifest strongly those characteristics we are arguing place a premium on intracompany as opposed to intercompany exchange.[18] It is beyond the scope of this study to evaluate the net benefits of Japanese policies toward technology transfers and foreign direct investment. It is suggestive, however, that there is some evidence that Japan is finding that the acquisition of more contemporary new-product technologies may require a change in its policies toward foreign ownership.[19]

Data indicate that non-trivial amounts of U.S. foreign ownership exist around the world in such manufacturing industries as food

---

servicing of a complicated machine require close coordination and planning. In each instance, an American manufacturer who has integrated across national boundaries may enjoy substantial advantages over one who has not and who can participate in foreign markets only through arms-length trading or licensing." (C. Fred Bergsten, Thomas Horst, and Theodore H. Moran, *American Multinationals and American Interests* [Washington, D.C.: The Brookings Institution, 1978], p. 234.)

[17] See T. Blumenthal, "Japan's Technological Strategy," *Journal of Development Economics*, No. 3, 1976, pp. 245-55.

[18] It is possible, of course, that differences between the Japanese and the Canadian direct investment experiences also reflect fundamental differences in entrepreneurial outlook, availability of risk capital, and other factors. Consideration of such factors is well outside the scope of this study.

[19] On these latter points, see Jack Behrman, *National Interests and the Multinational Enterprise* (Englewood Cliffs, N.J.: Prentice-Hall, 1970). A recent study of technology transfers from British to Indian firms concluded that attempts to secure local control over imported information through licensing agreements or joint ventures may simply reduce the incentives for foreign companies to provide assistance (see Howard Davies, "Technology Transfer Through Commercial Transactions," *Journal*

products, paper products, petroleum refining, and primary and fabricated metal products, as well as in primary resource industries and
in other non-manufacturing sectors. Such industries are not conventionally thought of as being technology-intensive. Thus, while
technological resources (which include associated marketing and
managerial skills) may be more efficiently transferred through intrafirm resource allocations than through market exchanges, it remains to be explained how the international extension of managerial
control increases the expected return on investment in industries not
necessarily characterized as being technology-oriented.

Other Advantages of Internal Organization[20]

Transactions Costs

The costs of effecting exchanges of either resources or finished
goods should be influenced by the characteristics of the resources or
goods being transferred. For example, market transfers of goods
characterized by a high degree of product differentiation could give
rise to the need for costly monitoring and quality-control procedures
among participants in arm's-length exchanges. Furthermore, disputes about product quality are more likely to arise in cases of
arm's-length exchanges of differentiated goods than in exchanges of
standardized products.[21] Market exchanges, or arm's-length transactions, will be potentially costly modes of organizing economic activity if the implementing of exchange agreements gives rise to costly
haggling among participants to the agreement and if non-compliance
with terms of the agreement is difficult to detect and punish. The
latter is more likely to occur when the characteristics of the commodities being exchanged are difficult to specify and/or measure.

An industry's market structure is also a potentially important
factor affecting the relative efficiency of market exchange compared
to intrafirm exchange. In this regard, oligopolistic market structures
may raise the costs of market exchange. For one thing, when there
are few buyers and sellers, price will be a negotiated, rather than an
externally determined, factor to market participants.[22] For another,
standards of reference regarding "fair" price and "representative"
quality are less readily available when there are few transactors in
a given industry. Finally, sellers (or buyers) may be more inclined to

---

of *Industrial Economics* 26, No. 2 [December, 1977]:161-75).

[20]The following discussion draws heavily upon ideas presented in Oliver E. Williamson, *Markets and Hierarchies: Analysis and Antitrust Implications* (New York: The
Free Press, 1975).

[21]Caves ("International Corporations," *op. cit.*) suggests that product differentiation
is the key to understanding horizontal foreign direct investment.

[22]Note that this does not necessarily imply that prices established in such markets
will be "non-competitive"; however, the costs of determining terms of exchange may
be higher in markets where there are few buyers and sellers than in markets where
there are many.

make factual misrepresentations, or even to repudiate original terms of an agreement, if alternatives facing them in the form of other potential partners to exchange are limited. The potential problems of small-numbers bargaining outlined above will be exacerbated if there is limited substitutability for the good or service being exchanged.

The potentially high cost of undertaking arm's-length exchange among a relatively small number of firms trading non-homogeneous goods and services offers a theoretical rationale for the observation that oligopoly with product differentiation normally prevails where corporations make horizontal investments abroad. Oligopoly, although not necessarily differentiated in the home market, is typical in industries undertaking vertical investments abroad.[23]

Access to Supplies

The potential importance of exchange costs, even in the absence of product differentiation, can be seen by recognizing that an important complementary input to financial investment in many industries (particularly in the resource sector) is long-term access to markets for the backward-linked supplier.[24] It is acknowledged that long-term marketing arrangements at pre-established prices reduce the risks associated with large-scale resource exploration and development. It has also been noted that better information about anticipated demand in forward-linked stages facilitates increased production efficiency in backward-linked stages of vertically integrated resource activities.[25] Therefore, access to long-term marketing contracts might be expected to increase the expected rate of return on investments in resource development activities.[26]

Independent resource producers and resource users could certainly agree to contract on a long-term basis; however, the costs of specifying, monitoring, and enforcing terms of the contract might be substantial. Successful long-term contracting between independent parties requires mutually agreed upon criteria for varying price and output. In practice, the parties might disagree as to whether actual conditions satisfied the contractual criteria for implementing changes in the terms of exchange, in which case recourse to expensive third-party arbitration might be required.[27] Indeed, if one party

---

[23] See Caves, "International Corporations," *op. cit.*

[24] Likewise, there are important advantages in having guaranteed long-term access to input supplies.

[25] This relationship is demonstrated in Kenneth Arrow, "Vertical Integration and Communication," *Bell Journal of Economics* 6, No. 1 (Spring, 1975):173-84.

[26] Indeed, such observers as Hugh G. J. Aitken (*American Capital and Canadian Resources* [Cambridge, Mass.: Harvard University Press, 1961], p. 85) cite the desire to secure access to lower-cost raw materials as the dominant motive for U.S. direct investment in Canadian resource industries.

[27] The recent example of Westinghouse Electric's refusal to supply uranium to nuclear-powered utility companies at contracted prices is a case in point. Westing-

to an exchange had substantial market power, it might simply choose to default on contracts that had become unfavorable in light of changing market conditions and to recoup any financial losses associated with its defaulting by monopoly pricing on new contracts. If parties to an exchange share common profit objectives, there is less reason to expect changing economic circumstances to precipitate contractual disputes. Even if divisions of the same firm disagree about terms of intrafirm exchange, the resolution of disputes through head-office decisions will ordinarily be a less costly way to resolve disagreements than will litigation.

In short, long-term contracting in the face of economic uncertainty can often be a costly and risky procedure. The risks and potential costs are presumably magnified by the problems of small-numbers bargaining that may arise in oligopolistic markets. Internalizing exchange activities within the firm might contribute to a lowering of costs associated with exchange agreements.

Economies of Scale

The economic advantages of extending managerial control over different activities will also depend upon the extent to which economies of scale can be realized. It has been argued that expanding firm size, particularly through centralization of certain management functions, provides opportunities for efficiency gains.[28] The existence of scale economies has been cited, particularly for such management functions as long-range planning, capital budgeting, and auditing, legal, and financial control.[29]

To be sure, managerial diseconomies of scale may set in beyond some critical firm size, particularly if larger firm size weakens the ability of the central office to ensure adherence by operating management to corporate-profit-maximization objectives. In this regard, the acquisition of additional foreign assets could contribute to reduced overall efficiency within the multinational corporation if the costs of head-office monitoring of a subsidiary's operating activities rise substantially.[30] Thus, the net advantage of coordinating inter-

---

house claimed that existing contracts to supply uranium were nullified by substantial, and unanticipated, increases in world uranium prices after contracts were signed. The utility companies, in turn, sued Westinghouse for breach of contract.

[28] Empirical evidence of the existence of synergy gains is somewhat less powerful than might be expected, given the ubiquity of the economies-of-scale argument. For a review of the literature in this area, see Peter O. Steiner, *Mergers: Motives, Effects, Policies* (Ann Arbor: University of Michigan Press, 1975).

[29] See Thomas Marx, "Internal Organization Structure and the FTC's Economic Report on Conglomerate Merger Performance," *Akron Business and Economic Review* 12, No. 3 (Winter, 1976):8-15.

[30] Williamson (*op. cit.*), among others, argues that the multi-divisional structure, characteristic of most large firms and particularly of multinational corporations, provides for superior compliance to overall corporate objectives on the part of operating units.

national economic activity through the international firm depends upon the extent to which managerial economies of scale outweigh any disadvantages created by expanding the network between central administration and operating personnel.[31]

Summary

The preceding discussion can be summarized as follows: every transfer of financial capital will inevitably be associated with a transfer of real resources — either embodied in the form of imported goods and services or disembodied in the form of technology licenses, purchased consulting services, and the like, or as part of a package of resources transferred through the multinational corporation via the direct investment route. All other things being the same, the preferred channel for transferring financial capital (that is, the channel promising the highest *ex ante* rate of return) will depend upon the costs associated with transferring desired real resources. The cost of transferring real resources through different channels (for example, arm's-length exchange or intrafirm exchange) will depend, in part, upon the nature of the resources being transferred and the structure of the markets in which exchange is undertaken. More specifically, the international extension of managerial control increases the efficiency with which resources are exchanged internationally when these resources are non-standardized (such as technological resources or managerial know-how) and when arm's-length exchange implies potential negotiating conflicts or foregone managerial economies of scale. To the extent that direct investment is, on average, a more efficient way of transferring resources under certain circumstances, alternative forms of foreign investment will not be perfect substitutes. Thus restrictions on foreign direct investment could be expected to reduce overall foreign investment in those activities where arm's-length exchange is less efficient than intracorporate exchange.

---

[31] It should be noted that firms may also realize unexploited economies of scale through further domestic, as opposed to international, diversification.

4

Empirical Analysis of U.S.
Foreign Direct Investment

Changes in the Geographical Distribution
of U.S. Foreign Direct Investment

Evaluations of the impact of foreign direct investment on the host economy should reflect the nature of those activities in which direct investment is a particularly preferred vehicle for transferring resources internationally. Existing studies of the impact of foreign investment in Canada tend to ignore distinctions among various forms of foreign investment. It will be argued later that an assumption that portfolio investment and direct investment are perfect substitutes leads to an understatement of the returns to foreign direct investment.[1]

In Technical Appendix A an attempt is made to evaluate empirically whether or not foreign direct investment is a preferred investment channel for specific economic activities. The analysis in that appendix provides some empirical support for the hypothesis that foreign direct investment by U.S. firms is a particularly favored means of exploiting competitive advantages in foreign markets, especially when these advantages are held in activities characterized as being technology-intensive and as taking place in concentrated market structures with concomitantly large average firm size. One important implication of this observation is that, while the Canadian tariff is an important factor influencing foreign direct investment in Canada (as we will demonstrate in a later section), it is not the only factor — or, necessarily, the most important factor — influencing foreign direct investment in specific Canadian industries. Thus elimination of the domestic tariff by itself would not necessarily encourage a substantial substitution of exporting activity for

---

[1] Consideration of whether higher returns to foreign direct investment reflect higher social as well as private returns (that is, whether the increased returns purely take the form of higher profits to the foreign investor) will be undertaken in a later section.

direct investment activity in various Canadian industries.[2] Another implication, which will be developed more completely later, is that the economic impact of foreign direct investment should be evaluated in light of its particular advantages for transferring resources in specific industries.

It might be argued, with some justification, that the empirical analysis summarized in Technical Appendix A is incomplete, since it ignores other factors that may have influenced the distribution of U.S. direct investment between Canada and other countries. Such factors include Canadian and European government policies toward foreign direct investment, changes in international exchange rates and in relative production costs for different countries, and reductions in tariff and non-tariff barriers to trade. Unfortunately, data required to account for all important determinants of U.S. direct investment patterns across countries are unavailable. Thus a more comprehensive approach to identifying the influence of specific variables on foreign direct investment, holding other variables (particularly those related to government policy) constant, might be to proceed by focusing on the distribution of U.S. foreign direct investment across Canadian manufacturing industries. This approach is undertaken in the next section.

Cross-Section Industry Studies of U.S. Direct Investment in Canada

Review of the Literature

Several studies have sought to identify the determinants of U.S. foreign direct investment in Canadian manufacturing industries. In one, Thomas Horst related U.S. exports plus subsidiary sales to Canada as a share of total Canadian imports plus total Canadian production, on the one hand, to R & D expenditures as a share of domestic sales in the United States, on the other, for 18 two-digit Canadian manufacturing industries in 1963. He found that R & D intensity was closely related to total U.S. sales to Canada and that U.S. exports as a share of total U.S. sales to Canada was negatively related to estimated nominal and effective tariff rates, as well as to the ratio of Canadian market size (Canadian production plus imports) to U.S. domestic production.[3]

In another study, Horst concluded that whether or not a U.S. manufacturing company owned a Canadian subsidiary depended

[2] The observation also provides an important qualification to the argument — made in André Raynauld, "The Ownership and Performance of Firms," in Gilles Paquet, ed., *The Multinational Firm and the Nation State* (Toronto: Ryerson Press, 1972), and elsewhere — that importing foreign products is always preferable to manufacturing them in domestic subsidiaries if the efficiency of the subsidiaries is not as high as that of the parent firm.
[3] See Thomas Horst, "The Industrial Composition of U.S. Exports and Subsidiary Sales to the Canadian Market," *American Economic Review* 62, No. 1 (March,

upon the industry in which the firm was located and upon the firm's size. The number of an industry's firms investing in Canada (holding size of firm constant) was positively related to an industry's R & D intensity and negatively related to the average asset size of foreign-owned subsidiaries in Canada. For 20 two-digit manufacturing industries the share of the Canadian industry's sales going to foreign-controlled firms was positively related both to industry R & D intensity and to the average asset size of foreign-owned subsidiaries in Canada. Thus industries in which economies of size are important apparently have fewer foreign investors controlling a larger share of the foreign market.[4]

Richard Caves investigated the determinants of the average share of sales accounted for by foreign-owned firms in the years 1965-67 for 64 Canadian manufacturing industries with respect to a host of independent variables. For the full sample of industries, he found that R & D expenditure as a percentage of sales was in all cases a significant variable, as was a measure of multi-plant economies of scale. While the percentage of shipments accounted for by large firms was always a statistically significant variable, Caves suggested that this variable might capture influences other than those it was supposed to measure. Other variables, including the effective tariff rate in Canada and relative wage costs in Canada and the United States, tended to be statistically insignificant.[5]

In a study cited earlier, H. G. Baumann measured the level of foreign direct investment in a Canadian industry by the shipments (sales) of U.S.-controlled subsidiaries divided by total shipments in Canada in 1968. Foreign direct investment was positively and significantly related to the proportion of professional and technical workers during 1961 in the comparable U.S. industry; the ratio of shipments from multi-plant enterprises to total shipments of the industry; the U.S. four-firm concentration ratio for the industry; and the average asset size of firms in the United States divided by the equivalent figure for Canadian-owned firms in the industry. Cost factors, advertising intensity, and the Canadian effective tariff rate were not significantly related to the extent of subsidiary production.[6]

In a recent study, Paul Gorecki found that domestic enterprises largely enter into industries with low barriers to entry, while

1972):37-46.

[4] See Thomas Horst, "Firm and Industry Determinants of the Decision to Invest Abroad: An Empirical Study," *Review of Economics and Statistics* 54, No. 3 (August, 1972):258-66.

[5] See Richard E. Caves, "Causes of Direct Investment: Foreign Firms' Shares in Canadian and United Kingdom Manufacturing Industries," *Review of Economics and Statistics* 56, No. 3 (August, 1974):279-93. Caves' finding that the tariff variable is statistically insignificant is consistent with evidence from other studies performed at the three-digit-industry level.

[6] See H. G. Baumann, "Merger Theory, Property Rights, and the Pattern of U.S.

foreign enterprises enter high- and low-barrier industries with approximately the same frequency. Furthermore, high advertising intensity and R & D intensity in an industry restricted the entry of
domestically owned firms into Canadian industries but did not re-
strict the entry of foreign-owned firms.[7]

Thus available cross-section studies of Canadian manufacturing
industries support, by and large, the suggested conclusions of Appendix Table A.1: foreign ownership is positively related to the
technological intensity and the optimal firm size in an industry.
There appears to be somewhat less consistent support for the notion
that foreign direct investment is positively related to industrial
concentration.

It should be noted that most of the empirical studies cited above
focus on the ratio of subsidiary sales to the value of domestic shipments as the dependent variable. This ratio will, in fact, reflect the
joint influence of two factors: the competitive advantage of foreign
firms in domestic markets and the degree to which foreign firms
exploit their competitive advantage through direct investment
abroad. Certain variables will be related to both factors. For example,
the importance of technological change, including changes in the
characteristics of industry output, to an industry's production process underlies the international competitive advantage of many U.S.
firms and, for reasons discussed in Chapter 3, also encourages these
firms to exploit their advantages in foreign markets by establishing
subsidiaries abroad, rather than by such arm's-length procedures as
exporting.[8] Thus existing studies for Canadian manufacturing industries do not provide unambiguous tests of the hypothesis that, given
some international competitive advantage, foreign firms' preferences
to exploit their advantage through foreign direct investment, rather
than through arm's-length exchanges, depend upon the nature of the
competitive advantage and the market structures of the industries
involved.

Some Additional Cross-Section Evidence

In order to identify more precisely the motives encouraging
foreign direct investment, an analysis of 29 two- and three-digit
Canadian manufacturing industries was undertaken in which the

Direct Investment in Canada," *Weltwirtschafliches Archiv* 3, No. 4 (1975):677-98.
[7] Paul Gorecki, "The Determinants of Entry by Domestic and Foreign Enterprises in
Canadian Manufacturing Industries: Some Comments and Empirical Results," *Review of Economics and Statistics* 58, No. 4 (November, 1976):485-88. Gorecki's
findings are supported by conclusions in Gideon Rosenbluth, "The Relation Between
Foreign Control and Concentration in Canadian Industry," *Canadian Journal of
Economics* 3, No. 1 (February, 1970):14-38.
[8] Other variables may not be directly related to both factors. For example, while the
domestic tariff should affect the decision of U.S. firms to establish subsidiaries in
Canada or to export, there is no reason to believe that Canadian tariffs are directly
related to the competitive advantages of U.S. firms.

dependent variable was the ratio of U.S. subsidiary sales to the sum of U.S. subsidiary sales and U.S. exports to Canada for a given industry in 1972.[9]

Besides taking into account the concentration ratio, average firm size, R & D intensity, and product differentiation activities in each sample industry, the dependent variable was related to a number of other potentially important factors. One of these was the level of tariffs. Presumably, the greater the barriers to trade in final goods, the greater the amount of trade that will be undertaken indirectly by relocating production — that is, investing abroad.[10] Another factor was the ratio of production costs in the United States to those in Canada. Presumably, relatively higher costs in the United States would, other things being constant, encourage U.S. firms to undertake production through the subsidiary route. Indeed, there is some evidence that relative increases in Canadian production costs have recently encouraged greater investment in the United States by Canadian companies. Unfortunately, precise measures of unit production costs in the two countries were unavailable for our sample industries. Relative costs of production were therefore measured as the ratio of the U.S. production wage rate to the Canadian production wage rate in each sample industry. A third factor was the extent of multi-plant economies in an industry. If there are cost advantages to operating a larger number of plants (for a given output volume), U.S. producers would be more likely, other things being the same, to supply the Canadian market from new plants established in Canada rather than from existing plants in the United States.

The dependent variable — the ratio of U.S. subsidiary sales to the sum of such sales and U.S. exports to Canada — was related to the set of independent variables, using multiple regression statistical techniques. The essential details of the exercise are contained in Technical Appendix B.[11] The main conclusions supported by this analysis can be summarized as follows:

• A high tariff rate in a domestic industry is a strong stimulant to greater foreign direct investment, relative to exporting, in the industry.

• The larger the average firm size in an industry and the higher the industrial concentration ratio, the greater the amount of

---

[9] Thus the dependent variable focuses directly upon the way in which the comparative advantages of U.S. firms are exploited in the Canadian economy. An exclusive focus upon the United States is not overly restrictive, since the bulk of foreign direct investment in Canada and of imports into Canada emanate from the United States.

[10] It should be noted, of course, that we are ignoring non-tariff barriers to trade, which may be important in certain industries. Unfortunately, ready empirical measures of non-tariff barriers are unavailable for Canada.

[11] Sources of data and other details of the analysis are available upon request from the author.

subsidiary production, relative to exporting, in the industry. Other factors positively related to the dependent variable include the ratio of scientists and engineers to total employees, which is used as a measure of R & D intensity; the ratio of advertising to sales in an industry, which is taken to be a measure of the extent to which product qualities and characteristics change over time; the wage rate of U.S. relative to Canadian production workers; and the extent of multi-plant economies of scale in an industry.

It must be noted that only the tariff variable was statistically significant at conventional confidence levels. Thus the regression analysis described in Appendix B provides, at best, directional support for the hypotheses proposed earlier. However, allowing for a variety of empirical problems associated with specifying variables of interest and with estimating equations, the results are, on balance, supportive of conclusions drawn from the analysis of U.S. export data. Furthermore, the impact of particular factors on the direct investment decision will vary across industries. Thus it is likely true that, while a number of the independent variables described above are only weakly related to the dependent variable across the entire sample of 29 industries, the statistical relationship would be observed to be much stronger in a given subset of industries.[12] With these empirical results in hand, we turn in the next chapter to a consideration of the economic impact of foreign direct investment on the country receiving that investment.

---

[12]This assertion is consistent with our earlier discussion and with the observation made in C. Fred Bergsten, Thomas Horst, and Theodore H. Moran, *American Multinationals and American Interests* (Washington, D.C.: The Brookings Institution, 1978), p. 234, that it is important to disaggregate when considering the impact of foreign direct investment.

Technical Appendix A

An Analysis of the Geographical Distribution of U.S. Foreign Direct Investment

One noteworthy feature of recent patterns of U.S. foreign direct investment is the substantially faster growth of such investment in Europe than in Canada. Over the period 1966-74 the value of U.S. foreign direct investment in Europe increased by about 172 percent, while the comparable increase for Canada was around 81 percent. The specific increases in the manufacturing sectors over the same period were 167 percent for Europe and 101 percent for Canada.[1] This technical appendix investigates whether recent patterns of U.S. foreign direct investment are consistent with the hypotheses raised about the potential advantages of foreign direct investment.

The underlying basis for the following analysis is the notion that product and factor flows are alternative ways of equalizing factor returns across countries.[2] The degree to which the export of commodities, of factors of production through arm's-length agreements (for example, through technology licenses), or of factors of production through foreign direct investment are substitute ways of exploiting a country's comparative trade advantages will depend, in part, upon the nature of the country's comparative advantage as well as upon the industrial organization of the relevant markets, as outlined in Chapter 3. Thus a country's geographical pattern of foreign direct investment should reflect its pattern of comparative advantages vis-à-vis other countries. More specifically, we noted in Chapter 2 that, over the period 1966-74, U.S. direct investment in European manufacturing industries increased relative to that in Canadian manufacturing industries. Our discussion of the foreign-direct-investment process in Chapter 3 suggested that the basis of U.S. trade with Europe as compared to Canada should reflect the following change over a similar period: potential U.S. exports of man-

---

[1] These rates are calculated from data in U.S. Department of Commerce, *Survey of Current Business* (Washington, D.C.: U.S. Government Printing Office, various issues).

[2] There is a substantial consensus in the theoretical and empirical literature that international resource and factor flows reflect underlying differences in countries' comparative advantages (see Richard E. Baldwin, "International Trade in Inputs and Outputs," *American Economic Review* 60, No. 2 [May, 1970]:430-35).

ufactured goods that can be characterized as technology-intensive or product-differentiated and originating in concentrated industries with above-average optimal firm sizes increased relatively more for Western Europe than for Canada.[3]

We have investigated whether the hypothesized changes in U.S. trade patterns were observable over the period 1961-72. Clearly, no direct measure of potential exports is available. We therefore examined changes in the actual composition of U.S. exports to Europe and Canada.[4] We gathered data on total U.S. exports, as well as U.S. exports to Western Europe and to Canada, for 19 two-digit manufacturing industries. For each year, 1961 to 1963, we calculated, for each of these industries, the percentage of total U.S. exports that went to Western Europe and to Canada and then averaged the percentages over the three years. We performed the same calculation for the period 1970-72. Changes in the composition of U.S. exports to different geographic areas are taken to reflect changes in the underlying demand for U.S. products in these areas.[5]

The use of actual export patterns as a measure of potential exports invites certain criticisms. If, for certain types of exports, production abroad and exporting are in some degree alternative ways of exploiting trade advantages, then actual exports may understate the trade advantages that the United States has in certain products by the amount of subsidiary production in these products. To some extent, this potential problem is offset by the use of lagged direct investment data — that is, we are seeking to establish that the relative increase in U.S. foreign direct investment in Europe compared to Canada over the period 1966-74 reflects a relative increase in European demand for U.S. products whose embodied resources are most efficiently transferred through the direct investment process, rather than through arm's-length processes such as exports financed indirectly by transfers of financial capital. If foreign direct investment responds with a lag to changing patterns of international demand, relative changes in export patterns for earlier periods may be

---

[3] Our analysis would obtain a greater level of generality if expenditures on licensing contracts and the like were compared, by industry, to exports and to foreign direct investments. Unfortunately, comprehensive data by detailed industry level are available only for the latter two categories.

[4] The sample of European countries included the United Kingdom, France, West Germany, Italy, the Netherlands, Austria, Switzerland, and Belgium/Luxembourg. These countries encompass the bulk of U.S. direct investment in Europe.

[5] The sample of industries was made up of food and beverages, tobacco, petroleum, chemicals, leather, rubber, wood, pulp and paper, textiles, non-metallic minerals, primary metals, fabricated metals, machinery, electrical equipment, aircraft and parts, other transportation equipment, furniture, clothing, and scientific instruments. The motor vehicles and parts industry was not included in the sample because the Canadian-U.S. automotive agreement has been such a strong influence on post-1965 trade patterns for this industry that the influence of other determinants of comparative advantage may be obscured.

reliable indicators of relative changes in underlying expected rates of return to foreign direct investment in subsequent periods.[6]

While our initial period (1961-63) and terminal period (1970-72) for calculating export intensities predate the initial period (1966) and the terminal period (1974) used for calculating relative changes in U.S. direct investment, there is a substantial time overlap between the two series.[7] As a result, changes in the calculated export intensities for certain goods will understate changes in international demand patterns to the extent that subsidiary production displaced exports during the overlapping time period.

The discussion in Chapter 3 suggests that we should observe the following pattern: over the sample period, U.S. exports to Europe of technology-intensive and/or product-differentiated manufactured goods produced in industries with above-average concentration levels (as a proxy for potential bargaining problems associated with small numbers of transactors) and above-average firm sizes increased relative to similar exports going to Canada.

The technological intensity of an industry was measured as the ratio of total R & D expenditures to total value of shipments for the industry in the base year 1967. An index of the technological intensity of U.S. exports of manufactured goods to Europe over the period 1961-63 was estimated as follows: the calculated technological intensity for each sample industry was multiplied by the percentage of total U.S. exports originating in each industry over the period. The product was, in turn, multiplied by the percentage of total U.S. exports originating in the industry that went to our sample of European countries. The calculated statistic was summed over the entire sample of 19 manufacturing industries and multiplied by 100, thereby providing an index value of the technological intensity of U.S. manufactured-goods exports to our sample of European countries. Similar index values were calculated for the technological intensity of manufactured goods exported to Europe over the period 1970-72 and for manufactured goods exported to Canada for the two sample periods.

Average firm size in an industry, employed as a proxy for optimal firm size, was obtained by dividing an industry's value of shipments by the total number of companies in the industry. Average concentration ratios for each industry were obtained from the industry's four-firm concentration ratio. In a manner analogous to the

---

[6] Such a lag is consistent with "product-life-cycle" models of international trade and investment. For a lucid description of the product-life-cycle model, see Raymond Vernon, "International Investment and International Trade in the Product Cycle," *Quarterly Journal of Economics* 80 (May, 1966):190-207.

[7] While our preference was to use export data for an earlier period, comprehensive export data for the United States on a "country-of-destination" basis are unavailable before 1961.

TABLE A.1

**Indexes, by Sample Characteristics, of U.S.
Exports to Europe Relative to U.S. Exports to Canada**[a]

	Canada			Europe		
	1961-63	1970-72	2÷1	1961-63	1970-72	2÷1
	(1)	(2)	(3)	(1)	(2)	(3)
Technological intensity	.473	.692	1.463	.684	1.470	2.149
			(1.528)			
Average firm size	55.560	66.480	1.197	88.030	137.770	1.565
		(69.47)	(1.250)			
Concentration	37.430	36.120	.965	40.960	55.100	1.345
		(37.74)	(1.008)			

[a]For 19 industries.

Source: See text.

way in which index values of the technological intensity of U.S. exports were calculated, index values of concentration and average firm size were calculated for U.S. exports to Europe and Canada. For example, the concentration index for U.S. exports to Europe was calculated by multiplying the concentration ratio for each sample industry by the percentage of total U.S. exports originating in the industry and, in turn, by multiplying the product by the percentage of U.S. exports to Europe that originated in the industry. Resulting values were summed over all industries and multiplied by 100.

The statistics obtained by the procedure described above are presented in Appendix Table A.1. Since the absolute values of the index numbers in any one of the sample years are less important than changes in the index values for the entire period, column 3 of the table provides the quotient of the index values for the beginning and terminal periods for Europe and Canada. Our hypotheses suggest that index values for the three characteristics investigated in Appendix Table A.1 should show relatively greater increases for Europe than for Canada. An investigation of the results described in Appendix Table A.1 shows that, indeed, index values for the technological intensity, average firm size, and industrial concentration of U.S. exports of manufactured goods to Europe increased faster than comparable indexes for those to Canada.

Since U.S. exports to Europe for the full 19-industry sample underlying Appendix Table A.1 grew at a faster rate than exports to Canada over the sample period, observed changes in the index values will reflect relative changes in the mix of exports to Europe and Canada as well as in the growth of total exports to each area. It would be interesting to evaluate the separate influences of these changes on the calculated index values. We proceed by noting that

the average value of U.S. exports to Canada of manufactured goods
— excluding those of the motor vehicle industry — as a percentage
of the value of total U.S. manufactured-goods exports increased from
16.2 percent for the period 1961-63 to 19.6 percent for the period
1970-72. Comparable values for Europe are 20.2 percent and 28.1
percent. Thus exports to Europe increased by approximately 4.5 percentage points more than exports to Canada. The faster relative
growth in overall manufactured exports to Europe was "held constant" by multiplying the calculated Canadian index values for
1970-72 (provided in Appendix Table A.1) by the factor 1.045. The
resulting values, shown in parentheses under the original estimates
in that table, may be thought of as the Canadian index values that
would have been realized had U.S. exports to Canada grown at the
same rate as exports to Europe, given the actual product mix of U.S.
exports to Canada over the sample period. It can be seen that column 3 values for Canada are little changed after the adjustment described above. Thus relative changes in the composition of U.S. exports to Europe and Canada may be considered the major source of
observed changes in the index values for the two regions. This observation is quite enlightening, inasmuch as some observers have
argued that relative shifts in patterns of U.S. direct investment
largely reflect faster economic growth in Western Europe compared
to Canada since 1950.[8]

---

[8] See, for example, Irving Brecher, *Capital Flows Between Canada and the United States* (Montreal: Private Planning Association of Canada, 1965), p. 22.

5

Impact of Foreign Direct Investment on the Host Country

In the introduction to this study the hypothesis was put forward that, in certain industries, foreign direct investment is a preferred means of transferring production resources internationally. In theory, Canada could borrow money abroad to acquire foreign factors of production either already embodied in goods and services (in the form of imports) or disembodied in the form of explicit factor flows (for example, through technology licenses and foreign engineering and management consulting services). If, for any combination of reasons, it is easier, or less costly, to transfer resources as part of a direct investment package, attempts to encourage the substitution of portfolio investment for direct investment will, other things being constant, reduce the total inflow of foreign production resources into Canada. The empirical results cited above are consistent with the notion that, in certain industries, direct investment and trade in finished goods are imperfect substitutes.[1] Moreover, there is some reason to argue that this is so particularly in those industries characterized by above-average rates of technological change (including product improvements) and by the presence of firm-level economies of scale. The former point is supported by the observation that foreign direct investment is a preferred means of exploiting competitive advantage in those industries with above-average rates of R & D and advertising expenditure. The latter point is supported by the finding that foreign direct investment is concentrated in industries of above-average firm size with concomitantly high industrial concentration ratios.[2]

Some observers might dispute the claim that advertising intensity is an appropriate measure of improvement in product quality and, therefore, that any restrictions on incoming foreign direct investment will reduce rates of investment in those industries

---

[1] Unfortunately, it was not possible to consider the degree to which foreign direct investment and the arm's-length purchase of disembodied factors of production are imperfect substitutes.

[2] These conclusions are put forward cautiously in light of the weak statistical evidence described in Appendix B.

particularly marked by above-average rates of technological change embodied in product improvements. They would argue that a substantial amount of advertising is devoted primarily to altering demand conditions. According to this view, restrictions on foreign direct investment may promote competition by reducing "artificial" product differences and by encouraging foreign firms to substitute price for non-price competition.[3] It should be noted, however, that at least one study has found advertising expenditures to be more significant in explaining foreign ownership levels in Canadian producer-goods than in Canadian consumer-goods industries.[4] It seems unlikely that the bulk of advertising expenditures in producer-goods industries is "image"-oriented rather than information-oriented.

It might also be argued that the concentration of foreign direct investment in oligopolistic industries containing firms of above-average size is evidence that foreign firms make investments in the host economy to realize monopoly profits rather than to take advantage of inherent scale economies. More specifically, foreign firms might seek to eliminate large, domestically owned firms in order to obtain monopolistic positions in domestic markets. Some specific evidence bearing on this argument will be presented later. It is merely noted at this point that the preponderance of foreign direct investment takes place by internal expansion rather than by external expansion (that is, by acquisition). Furthermore, most foreign acquisitions involve takeovers of relatively small firms, which are unlikely to provide foreigners with enhanced market power in domestic industries.

Some Empirical Estimates

One well-known attempt (by Rudolph Penner) to measure the benefits of foreign investment in Canada views these benefits as arising primarily from the addition to Canada's capital stock; no distinction is made between the potential impact of direct versus portfolio investment.[5] Furthermore, it is assumed that, while some new technical knowledge is implemented by foreign investment, it is no greater than the amount that would be implemented by an equivalent level of domestic investment. Simplifying assumptions are also made that the technological change associated with foreign

---

[3] This view has been put forth in H. Edward English, "Canada-United States Relations," *Proceedings of the Academy of Political Science* 2 (1976): 68-79.

[4] See Richard E. Caves, "Causes of Direct Investment: Foreign Firms' Shares in Canadian and United Kingdom Manufacturing Industries," *Review of Economics and Statistics* 56, No. 3 (August, 1974): 286.

[5] See Rudolph Penner, "The Benefits of Foreign Investment in Canada, 1950 to 1956," *Canadian Journal of Economics and Political Science* 32, No. 2 (May, 1966):172-83. Since U.S. direct investment as a ratio of the total value of foreign investment averaged approximately .85 over Penner's sample period, his analysis is essentially applicable to the benefits of U.S. direct investment in Canada.

investment proceeds at the same rate as that associated with domestic investment, that techniques introduced by foreigners have no external effects, and that the average propensity to consume in Canada is constant and remains unaffected by foreign investment.

Assuming that new technology is embodied in the capital-formation process, Penner concludes that elimination of net foreign investment from 1950 to 1956 would have resulted in a decline of $1,082 million (or 6 percent) in non-agricultural, non-residential gross domestic product, to $17,003 million in 1949 dollars. When an adjustment is made for reduced foreign investment payments to foreigners, the calculated benefit of foreign investment amounts to $771 million. This implies a reduction in Canadian gross domestic product of about 3.25 percent over the sample period.[6] Put in perspective, the embodiment assumption gives rise to an estimated benefit of $56 per capita in 1956 dollars over the sample period. If technology is assumed to be entirely disembodied, the elimination of foreign investment over the period 1950-56 would have reduced Canadian gross domestic product by an estimated $336 million, or about 1.4 percent.[7] This study would therefore imply that a relatively small benefit is to be realized from foreign investment.

A more recent study by T. L. Powrie concludes, on the basis of an analysis of the period 1950-76, that, if Canada's net international indebtedness had not been allowed to grow at all after January 1, 1950, the country's national income in 1976 would have been, at worst, lower by an amount equal to six months' normal growth.[8] The author employs a number of models to estimate the impact of foreign investment. The model he favors allows for some substitution of domestic savings for foreign savings in the event that the supply of foreign loans is shut off; however, it is assumed that the productivity of foreign-direct-investment capital is equal to the average productivity of all capital in the Canadian economy, that foreign direct investment imparts no "spillover" economic benefits to domestic factors of production, and that the average propensity to consume in the Canadian economy is unaffected by foreign investment.

Various studies therefore suggest the fundamental conclusion that the economic cost to Canadians of reduced foreign direct investment may be relatively small. Given the potential significance of

---

[6]*Ibid.*, p. 178.

[7]*Ibid.*, p. 180. This estimate is put into perspective when it is recognized that recent estimates of the gains to Canada from free trade with the United States are about 8.2 percent of GNP in 1974 (see D. J. Daly and S. Globerman, *Tariff and Science Policies: Applications of a Model of Nationalism*, Ontario Economic Council Research Study Number 4 [Toronto: University of Toronto Press, 1976], p. 29).

[8]See T. L. Powrie, "The Contribution of Foreign Capital to Canadian Economic Growth," mimeographed, Department of Economics, University of Alberta, July, 1977, p. 1. References are also provided there to other estimates of the impact of foreign investment in Canada.

such a conclusion to public policies affecting bilateral capital flows, it is important to consider the magnitude and direction of any potential biases in existing studies. Such biases may arise from the failure to recognize the distinctive nature of foreign direct investment.

Productivity of Foreign Direct Investment

We suggested earlier that foreign direct investment might be more productive than other forms of capital formation. More specifically, technological change — particularly improvements in product quality — associated with foreign direct investment may, on average, proceed at a faster rate than that associated with domestic investment. Furthermore, foreign direct investment may facilitate the capture of economies of scale if foreigners can more efficiently manage firms of larger average size. Some evidence — although largely indirect — is available to support these assertions. For example, it has been found that, for a sample of 2,000 manufacturing establishments located in Quebec in 1961, value added per worker in a foreign-owned plant was approximately 1.5 times the value added per worker in an English Canadian-owned plant and about 1.8 times the value added per worker in a French Canadian-owned plant.[9] Recent evidence provided by Statistics Canada data indicates that value added per employee is higher in U.S.-controlled than in Canadian-controlled plants for an overwhelming majority of Canadian manufacturing industries.[10] The precise sources of the labor-productivity advantages of foreign-owned plants are not identified in the above-mentioned studies; therefore, it cannot necessarily be concluded that total factor productivity is higher in foreign-owned plants. Indeed, these studies indicate that foreign-owned establishments are substantially larger and more capital-intensive than domestically owned plants, which would contribute to higher labor productivity in foreign-owned plants.

When firm size is held constant, there is no evidence of any consistent relation between unit production costs and ownership.[11] However, for any particular overall firm size, unit production costs will be influenced, in part, by the degree of product diversity. It has been found that foreign-owned plants of any given size are more diversified than those belonging to domestically owned Canadian companies.[12] The additional product diversification undertaken by subsidiaries undoubtedly raises production costs in the subsidiary.

---

[9] See André Raynauld, "The Ownership and Performance of Firms," in Gilles Paquet, ed., *The Multinational Firm and the Nation State* (Toronto: Ryerson Press, 1972).

[10] Statistics Canada, *Foreign Ownership and Control of Canadian Manufacturing Establishments* (Ottawa, 1977).

[11] See A. E. Safarian, *Foreign Ownership of Canadian Industry* (Toronto: McGraw-Hill, 1966), p. 259.

[12] Richard E. Caves, *Diversification, Foreign Investment and Scale in North American Manufacturing Industries* (Ottawa: Information Canada, 1975).

These observations imply that foreign-owned firms of a given size might be observed to have lower unit production costs than domestically owned firms of the same size if domestically owned firms produced as diverse an array of output as foreign-owned firms typically do. A further implication is that any superior efficiency of foreign subsidiaries is, in part, passed on to Canadian consumers in the form of greater product variety and — possibly — superior product quality.[13]

Additional indirect evidence on the productivity performance of foreign-owned versus domestically owned firms is provided in several studies of R & D performance and the adoption of new technology in Canada. One recent study found that foreign-owned firms in the electrical industry obtained fewer patents for any given level of R & D spending than did domestically owned firms, while the relationship of R & D to patents was unrelated to ownership in the chemical and machinery industries.[14] The results suggest that, in relation to dollars spent, foreign-owned firms may not provide superior R & D performances within Canada; however, one might well question the propriety of using patents as a measure of R & D output, particularly in view of the possibility that foreign subsidiaries allow their parent firms to patent a product worldwide if there are substantial economies of scale in so doing. A study of the Canadian tool and die industry found that, holding other factors constant, domestically owned and foreign-owned firms adopted numerically controlled machine tools at approximately the same rate.[15] In contrast, it was determined that domestically owned firms were significantly slower to adopt a process innovation (involving special presses) in the paper industry than were foreign-owned firms,[16] while a study of the Canadian appliance industry suggests that foreign-owned firms were in the forefront of adapting new products developed abroad to local production conditions.[17]

The evidence is far from conclusive, and much of it is indirect; however, it suggests that, within particular Canadian industries, foreign subsidiaries are, on average, more efficient than domestically

[13] One can, of course, argue about whether greater product diversification is a desirable way to use the efficiency benefits of foreign direct investment. It might be suggested, however, that the establishment of conditions under which more price, and less non-price, competition is undertaken in domestic industries is more appropriately a concern of domestic competition policy.

[14] Donald McFetridge, *Government Support of Scientific Research and Development: An Economic Analysis*, Ontario Economic Council Research Study Number 8 (Toronto: University of Toronto Press, 1977).

[15] Steven Globerman, "Technological Diffusion in the Canadian Tool and Die Industry," *Review of Economics and Statistics* 57, No. 4 (November, 1975):428-34.

[16] Steven Globerman, "New Technology Adoption in the Canadian Paper Industry," *Industrial Organization Review* 4 (1976):5-12.

[17] Harold Crookell, "The Role of Product Innovation in Trade Flows," mimeographed, School of Business Administration, University of Western Ontario, London, 1970.

owned firms. To the extent that this is valid, existing studies may have underestimated the benefits of foreign direct investment by weighting foreign capital's contribution to output by the average return to both foreign-owned and domestically owned capital.[18]

Impact of Foreign Direct Investment on Domestic Savings

Available estimates of the impact of foreign direct investment on Canada's economic growth assume that the domestic average propensity to save is not directly affected by foreign investment rates. However, if, on balance, foreign direct investment stimulates domestic capital formation, existing estimates of the contribution of foreign investment may understate the true contribution by ignoring the positive indirect influence on domestically owned investment. Since a detailed consideration of this important issue would take us somewhat far afield, we merely note some relevant evidence bearing on the relationship between foreign ownership and domestic savings.

Caves and Reuber investigated the degree to which U.S. direct investment in Canada is merely a substitute for Canadian investment, thereby providing no net addition to Canada's capital stock. Based upon the period 1951-62, they concluded that, on average, a dollar's worth of direct investment can be associated with about two dollars of capital formation. The impact of the inflow is particularly marked during periods of vigorous economic activity. During deflationary periods a dollar of foreign direct investment is associated with only about 80 cents of capital formation in Canada.[19] A more recent study by Frances Van Loo qualifies the Caves and Reuber findings by considering both the direct and the indirect effects of foreign direct investment on capital formation in Canada. Van Loo found that over the period 1948-66 the total impact of foreign direct investment on domestic capital formation was probably smaller than the direct effect estimated by Caves and Reuber.[20]

Low estimates of the contribution of foreign investment to Canada's real economic growth usually include an assumption that additional domestic investment arises primarily from higher domestic saving — which is, in turn, derived from higher domestic income. Since the contribution of foreign direct investment to higher domestic income is deemed to be quite modest in such studies, the derived impact on domestic saving is, perforce, deemed to be modest. However, the evidence cited above suggests that foreign direct investment tends to stimulate domestic investment at any given income

[18] In more technical terms, existing studies may have underestimated the intramarginal returns to foreign direct investment by using marginal valuations to impute total benefits.

[19] Richard E. Caves and Grant Reuber, *Capital Transfers and Economic Policy: Canada, 1951-1962* (Cambridge, Mass.: Harvard University Press, 1971).

[20] Frances Van Loo, "The Effect of Foreign Direct Investment on Investment in Canada," *Review of Economics and Statistics* 59, No. 4 (November, 1977):474-81.

level, which therefore moves the Canadian economy onto a higher growth path than would otherwise be attained.[21]

Indirect Effects of Foreign Direct Investment

Yet another, and potentially important, source of downward bias in most studies yielding low estimates of the total economic benefits of foreign investment in Canada is the assumption that foreign investment has no indirect effects upon the productivity of domestically owned firms. However, a number of indirect, or external, spillover benefits from foreign direct investment have been hypothesized in the literature. For example, it has been argued that foreign direct investment increases competition among domestic producers, thereby encouraging greater efficiency in domestically owned firms. It has also been suggested that foreign direct investment stimulates domestically owned firms to adopt new technology faster, and to improve managerial practices sooner, than they otherwise would. Furthermore, many young managers and other workers trained in U.S. subsidiaries may transfer to domestically owned firms, thereby providing Canadian companies with "free" human capital.

On the other hand, it has been argued that the centralization of substantive managerial decision-making in multinational head offices encourages a net migration of talented managers and technicians from Canada, thereby reducing productivity throughout the economy.[22] Foreign direct investment also allegedly contributes to reduced innovation and low productivity in the Canadian economy by contributing to the existence of too many firms of below-optimal size producing too diverse an array of output and by restraining competition among foreign firms selling in the Canadian market.[23]

Whether positive external benefits accrue to foreign direct investment is ultimately an empirical question. Virtually no direct evidence on this issue has been obtained for Canada, although a study by Richard Caves suggests that such indirect benefits are difficult to identify.[24] The premise underlying his estimates of the indirect economic benefits of foreign direct investment is that, if

---

[21] It should be noted that, if foreign investment causes Canadian-financed investment to rise and if the economy is at full employment, some sacrifice of current consumption is implied.

[22] Somewhat dated evidence suggests that there is no pattern of discrimination by U.S. subsidiaries in favor of hiring Americans in technical and professional jobs in Canada; however, Canadianization is much less well-established in executive and policy-making positions (see John Lindeman and Donald Armstrong, *Policies and Practices of United States Subsidiaries in Canada* [Montreal and Washington, D.C.: Canadian-American Committee, 1961], p. 35).

[23] A summary of the various arguments can be found in Government of Canada, *Foreign Direct Investment in Canada* (Ottawa, 1972), which also discusses the indirect political and cultural impact of foreign direct investment.

[24] Richard E. Caves, "Multinational Firms, Competition, and Productivity in Host-Country Markets," *Economica* 41, No. 162 (May, 1974):176-91.

foreign investment contributes to increased allocative efficiency, the profit rates of domestically owned firms should be inversely related to the competitive pressure supplied by foreign firms, all other factors held constant. For a sample of 49 Canadian manufacturing industries, Caves' dependent variable was the average profit before taxes on equity over the period 1965-67 for corporations with less than 50 percent foreign ownership. The competitive pressure supplied by foreign firms was measured by subsidiaries' shares of sales as well as by subsidiaries' shares of assets in an industry. When other important explanatory variables were included in the basic statistical equation, the two share variables were unrelated to the dependent variable. Thus Caves' results do not provide any real support for the argument that foreign direct investment in Canada has "spillover" efficiency benefits.

The use of a profit-rate variable as an indirect measure of productivity might be criticized on the grounds that accounting profit rates are an unstable measure of industry performance and that interindustry differences in profit rates may vary substantially over the business cycle. Furthermore, one can imagine the existence of productivity spillovers that both reduce costs in domestically owned firms and increase industry competition. In such cases the external economic benefits of foreign direct investment might escape measurement if profitability is employed as the dependent variable. In the light of the unsatisfactory evidence available to date, a more direct test for the existence of spillover benefits from foreign direct investment was undertaken.[25]

The sample used for this test consisted of 61 Canadian manufacturing industries. The main results, obtained through statistical analysis, can be summarized as follows:

- Labor-productivity levels in domestically owned plants are positively, and significantly, related to capital intensity, plant-level economies of scale, and the degree of foreign production in an industry.

- To a lesser extent, labor productivity is also positively related to average work hours per employee and to labor quality in the plant.

- The effects on productivity of foreign-direct-investment spillovers are modest in comparison to those of increasing the amount of capital employed per worker; however, they are quite comparable to the productivity benefits arising from expanding plant size.

---

[25] A brief description of the methodology used in this study is contained in Technical Appendix C. A full description of the study is provided in Steven Globerman, "Foreign Direct Investment and 'Spillover' Efficiency Benefits in Canadian Manufacturing Industries," *Canadian Journal of Economics* 12, No. 1 (February, 1979):42-56.

These results provide an additional basis for arguing that studies may underestimate the true net benefits of foreign direct investment in Canada. Specifically, existing studies have ignored the possibility that foreign ownership stimulates greater efficiency in domestically owned firms.

Recapitulation

The relevance of the analysis to this point might be viewed in the following framework. Concern with high levels of foreign ownership has led many Canadians to consider whether access to foreign factors of production might be obtained without sacrificing additional domestic ownership and control of Canadian businesses — that is, whether portfolio borrowing to finance either imports of finished goods or purchases of foreign resources might be substituted for foreign direct investment. Conceptual and empirical analysis suggests, however, that foreign direct investment and foreign indirect investment are imperfect substitutes. Thus, for any given rate of return to foreign investment in the host country, attempts to substitute portfolio investment for direct investment will reduce the inflow of foreign capital, all other things remaining constant. The issue that then arises is the seriousness of any given reduction in foreign investment for the host economy. Available estimates for Canada suggest that the impact on economic growth of rather substantial reductions in foreign investment may be relatively small; however, there are good reasons to argue that these estimates understate the true impact that foreign direct investment has had on Canada's economic growth.[26]

---

[26] Unfortunately, no alternative specific estimate of the impact can be offered in this study. The suggestion is made that further investigation of the growth impact of foreign direct investment is warranted.

6

Bilateral Direct Investment: A Policy Overview

From the standpoint of public policy the precise contribution to growth from incremental foreign direct investment is not of direct concern. If all the growth benefits of such investment are captured by foreigners, the host government has no particular reason, based strictly on economic criteria, to favor or disfavor additional foreign direct investment. Thus the concern of policy-makers in the host country is more appropriately addressed to the question, Do the economic benefits not directly captured by the foreign investor exceed the economic, and non-economic, costs associated with foreign direct investment that are borne by home-country citizens? Available evidence discussed above suggests that some of the economic benefits of foreign direct investment have been captured by Canadians. These take the form of improved productivity in domestically owned establishments, wider selection of consumer goods (for any given cost), improved product quality in various industries, and higher wages for domestic workers, among other things.[1] Whether the net external economic benefits of foreign direct investment have exceeded real (or imagined) non-economic external costs in Canada is beyond the scope of this paper. However, one can at least conclude that the rationalization for restrictions on foreign direct investment in Canada must be based on non-economic criteria, since such restrictions impose net economic costs upon Canadians.

A substantial amount of debate in the United States has focused on the parallel question of whether direct investment abroad by U.S. companies provides net benefits or net costs to the U.S. economy. The criteria for evaluating the effects of this investment include employment opportunities for U.S. workers, balance of payments implications, and returns to capital. While it is difficult to summarize adequately the extensive literature in this area, it would appear reasonable to conclude that, on balance, U.S. direct investment

---

[1] Data in Statistics Canada, *Foreign Ownership and Control of Canadian Manufacturing Establishments* (Ottawa, 1977), indicate that, in the majority of Canadian manufacturing industries, production wages per employee are higher in foreign-owned plants than in domestically owned plants.

abroad has had a positive impact upon U.S. exports and upon domestic investment and employment.[2]

It should be noted that the assessment above is not beyond criticism and certainly cannot necessarily be applied to U.S. investment in all countries. For example, one study concludes that, while some domestic effects of U.S. foreign direct investment are clearly positive or negative, most appear to be roughly neutral.[3] Another suggests a distinctly non-neutral domestic economic impact of U.S. direct investment in Canada.[4] It concludes that the after-tax rate of return on domestic capital investment exceeded the after-tax rate of return on foreign direct investment in Canada when the latter was adjusted for exchange-rate changes. In this regard, it is interesting to note that studies of the impact of overseas direct investment on the British economy support the notion that the direct financial returns to the home country are relatively low: the continuing return to the British economy from overseas investment was found to be between £4 and £6 annually per £2,100 invested.[5] These findings call into question the notion that foreign direct investment is undertaken with the expectation of earning monopoly profits in foreign markets by creating, or exacerbating, non-competitive conditions in them.

Public-policy guidelines for evaluating the social benefits of direct investment abroad are conceptually the same as those for evaluating incoming foreign direct investment: Are the social benefits of the incremental investment greater than the social costs? Within this framework, existing findings are of limited usefulness, since they do not include estimates of any indirect benefits of foreign direct investment to the home country, although they are consistent with suggestions in the literature that, in the absence of constraints, U.S. firms will overinvest abroad. In brief, it has been argued that, in evaluating potential investments, U.S. firms investing abroad will not take into account the possible decrease in rates of return to other U.S. investments in an area. However, it might be pointed out that the investing firms will also ignore indirect benefits accruing to other domestic factors of production as a result of their decisions.

The existence of such benefits as favorable changes in terms of trade and reductions in domestic rates of inflation (by substituting lower-cost production abroad for domestic production) may contribute to underinvestment abroad by U.S. firms.[6] Furthermore, empirical

---

[2] Some evidence is provided in Business International Corporation, *The Effects of U.S. Corporate Foreign Investment, 1960-1972* (New York, 1974).

[3] C. Fred Bergsten, Thomas Horst, and Theodore H. Moran, *American Multinationals and American Interests* (Washington, D.C.: The Brookings Institution, 1978).

[4] H. G. Grubel, "Taxation and the Rates of Return from Some U.S. Asset Holdings Abroad, 1960-1969," *Journal of Political Economy* 82, No. 3 (May/June, 1974):469-89.

[5] See James W. C. Tomlinson, *The Joint-Venture Process in International Business* (Cambridge, Mass.: M.I.T. Press, 1970), p. 4.

[6] A more detailed consideration of the external costs and benefits of foreign direct

studies of the welfare effects of foreign direct investment on the home country have ignored potential benefits arising from international diversification of investment. Investment abroad may enable U.S. firms to reduce the expected variance of returns earned on any set of investments.[7] While there are reasons to discount the magnitude of potential diversification gains to U.S. firms investing in Canada (given a large and liquid domestic capital market and the opportunity to diversify internationally by making portfolio investments), potential gains exist in principle, given exchange-rate risk and less than full mobility of the factors of production.

Indirect domestic benefits from U.S. direct investment abroad may also arise from any political gains provided by international economic integration. Indirect "political" benefits from foreign direct investment by U.S. firms may, in fact, reduce costs that would otherwise have to be undertaken by the U.S. government because of the United States' role as leader of the free world. Such potential benefits include, for example, the enhanced political stability of recipient countries resulting from higher real incomes, greater stability of foreign-currency regimes by decentralizing foreign-dollar holdings,[8] increased cooperation worldwide on reducing trade and investment barriers, and a sharing of common objectives and perceptions of economic problems among free-world countries.

One might argue that a rising tide of nationalism (both in Canada and elsewhere) directed against international business has actually created political costs for the United States in terms of hostility toward U.S. government policy initiatives. Furthermore, foreign direct investment has imposed costs on both the Canadian and the U.S. governments in requiring bilateral agreements on tax treaties, transfer-pricing policies, and periodic governmental interfacing on the extraterritorial application of foreign legislation. But even though precise estimates of the political benefits and costs of foreign direct investment to the home country are probably impossible to obtain, the strong support of the U.S. government for international capital mobility suggests that net benefits may exist.

---

investment to the home country is provided in the accompanying monograph in this volume.

[7] Some recent empirical evidence on this point is provided in Sheldon Novack, "An Empirical Test of the Benefits of International Investment," *American Economist* 20, No. 1 (Spring, 1976): 44-51.

[8] In light of the recent situation of a rapidly depreciating U.S. dollar, it is difficult to keep in mind that, in the not too distant past, a major concern of Western European countries was the shortage of U.S. dollars as an international medium of exchange.

7

Conclusion

The decreasing relative importance of bilateral direct investment in the overall international allocation of investment capital
suggests the possibility that private rates of return to bilateral direct investment have decreased. It is also possible that social rates of
return to bilateral direct investment have decreased. From a
public-policy standpoint, however, the absolute rates of return to
foreign direct investment from the perspectives of the host and the
home countries are not directly relevant. As long as the benefits of
U.S. direct investment in Canada (or of Canadian direct investment
in the United States) exceed the costs for residents of both the host
and the home countries, economic-policy criteria call for the Canadian and U.S. governments to encourage rather than discourage increased bilateral direct investment.

While a precise accounting of the total costs and benefits of direct investment has yet to be undertaken, a judicious interpretation
of the evidence presented in this monograph and elsewhere suggests
that the international reallocation of factors of production effected
through the direct investment process has provided net economic benefits for both the investing and the recipient countries. To be sure,
the observation that the total benefits of foreign direct investment
have exceeded the total costs says little about the net benefits of
foreign direct investment at the margin — that is, it does not necessarily follow that the economic benefits foregone from relatively
small decreases in rates of growth of foreign direct investment will
be substantial. However, the foregoing analysis does imply that
policies encouraging a substantial reduction in rates of growth of
bilateral direct investment may impose significant economic costs
upon the host and, possibly, the home countries, all other things
being equal. Furthermore, there is reason to believe that future capital requirements call for accelerated investment in activities that
manifest a distinct preference for direct, as opposed to portfolio, investment.[1] Unilateral (or bilateral) restrictions on foreign direct

---

[1] For example, future capital requirements in both countries appear to call for heavy
investment in such sectors as the extraction of energy resources and the development

investment could conceivably reduce the overall rate of net capital formation in these and other areas in which both Canada and the United States have important stakes in encouraging intensified economic activity.

---

of technology-intensive hydrocarbon substitutes. For reasons outlined in this study, both types of activities manifest a distinct preference for foreign direct, as opposed to portfolio, investment.

Technical Appendix B

Determinants of Exporting Versus
Subsidiary Selling in U.S. Companies

The dependent variable employed in this appendix is defined as the ratio in 1972 of subsidiary sales in Canada made by U.S.-owned companies (S_i) to the sum of S_i plus U.S. exports to Canada (E_i). The following independent variables were included in various combinations in the regression equations that were estimated:

C_i = four-firm concentration ratio in the ith U.S. industry in 1967.

A_i = value of shipments, in millions of U.S. dollars, divided by the number of companies in the ith U.S. industry in 1967.

M_i = number of establishments divided by the number of companies in the ith U.S. industry in 1967. This variable is taken to be a measure of the extent of multi-plant economies of scale.

NT_i, ET_i = nominal and effective Canadian tariff rates for the ith industry in 1963.

T_i = total number of scientists and engineers divided by total employment in the ith U.S. industry in 1970. This variable is employed as a tentative measure of the R & D intensity of an industry.

P_i = advertising expenditures in Canada as a percentage of value of shipments in Canada in the ith industry in 1965. This variable is taken to be a measure of the importance of product differentiation as a competitive tool in the sample industries.

Since the foreign-direct-investment decision is presumably undertaken with a lag, prior-year values are specified for the set of independent variables employed. No claim is made that the particular lags specified are optimal either theoretically or empirically. Indeed, the availability of requisite data in given years had much to do with the chosen specification of several independent variables. Since the variables are already in ratio form, a linear specification of the relationship between the dependent and the independent variables is appropriate. Besides affording easier comprehension, the linear specification provided better overall goodness of fit (by conventional measures) than did log-linear specifications. Very little difference in results was obtained employing either the nominal or the effective

48

tariff measures. Hence results are reported below only for the nominal tariff specification. We also report only the results of a number of estimated equations that are sufficient to illustrate the general results obtained.

Equation 1 shows results obtained when the dependent variable is estimated as a function of C_i, A_i, M_i, NT_i, and T_i. A t statistic is shown below each co-efficient; $\bar{R}^2$ is the adjusted (for degrees of freedom) co-efficient of determination. The equations are estimated for a sample of 29 two- and three-digit Canadian manufacturing industries.

1. $S_i/(S_i + E_i) = .5590 + .0007C_i + .0037A_i + .02354M_i +$
$$ (.41) \qquad (1.66) \qquad (.65)$$
$$+ .0100NT_i + .4237T_i$$
$$ (2.98) \qquad (.70)$$
$$\bar{R}^2 = .227$$

All the estimated parameters are positive, which is in accord with our theoretical expectations. However, only the nominal tariff variable is statistically significant at the .05 level. The equation is also plagued by potential multi-collinearity among the C_i, A_i, and M_i variables — that is, the simple correlation co-efficient between C_i and A_i is .32, while the co-efficient between A_i and M_i is .36. The relatively low $\bar{R}^2$ indicates that our independent variables explain only a small portion of the variance in our dependent variable.

It might be objected that the measure of R & D intensity chosen is inappropriate in that it fails to distinguish between technical processes of a conventional engineering nature and those involving rapid changes in the characteristics of products. The imperatives for internalizing the exchange of R & D resources should be more apparent in industries exhibiting the latter form of technological change. However, equation 2 indicates that little improvement is achieved in our statistical results when the technology variable is respecified as the advertising intensity in an industry.

2. $S_i/(S_i + E_i) = .5391 + .0006C_i + .0033A_i + .0082M_i +$
$$ (.34) \qquad (1.56) \qquad (.12)$$
$$+ .0089NT_i + .0090P_i$$
$$ (2.11) \qquad (.758)$$
$$\bar{R}^2 = .204$$

The parameter estimate for the P_i variable, while positive, is unreliable in that there is quite substantial intercorrelation between the NT_i and P_i variables; the simple correlation co-efficient equals .51.

Efforts were made to improve our overall statistical results by including a variable that attempted to capture the influence of cost-of-production differences between the two countries — that is, the ratio of the average production wage rate in U.S. manufacturing plants to the average production wage rate in Canadian manufacturing plants (expressed in U.S. dollars) in 1970. Furthermore, the overall sample was stratified into producer- and consumer-goods industries, and basic equations were estimated separately for the two samples. The motor vehicle and parts industry was dropped from the sample to eliminate the possibility that the auto pact distorts results for the overall sample. No substantive changes to our basic conclusions materialized from these procedures.

In summary, the statistical analysis described in this appendix provides, at best, directional support for the main hypotheses outlined in the text. It is conceivable that more precise specification of the relevant variables and alternative specifications of the basic empirical relationship would provide improved results. Furthermore, a larger sample could mitigate some of the multi-collinearity problems in the estimating equation. Such refinements are left to another study.

Technical Appendix C

An Empirical Analysis of
Indirect Productivity Benefits

The efficiency of domestically owned plants, our dependent variable (V_i), was measured directly as the ratio of total value added, in thousands of Canadian dollars, to the total number of employees for 1972. This partial productivity measure will be analyzed as a function of a number of independent variables, including differences in factor proportions, quality of inputs, economies of scale, and technological efficiency. Since capital and labor are complementary inputs, value added per employee will be positively related to the ratio of capital services to labor services. In the absence of detailed capital-stock data for disaggregated Canadian industries, the ratio of the gross book value of depreciable assets at the end of 1971 to the total number of employees in 1972 (K_i) for a comparably defined U.S. industry was employed as a proxy for the capital/labor ratio in Canadian-owned plants in a given industry.

Differences in measured labor productivity in domestically owned plants will also be influenced by differences in labor quality. As a result of the potential least-squares bias associated with using measured average wages as a proxy for labor quality, a number of alternative instrumental variables were employed. In one case, the ratio in 1972 of total salaries and wages to the total number of employees in foreign-owned plants in the ith Canadian industry (L_{1i}) was used as a measure of average labor quality in domestically owned plants in the same industry. An alternative exogenous measure employed was the percentage of total male employees who had some university education or a university degree in the ith Canadian industry in 1971 (L_{2i}). A third approach involved the use of a two-stage least-squares estimation, where the instrument (L_{3i}) was obtained as the forecast value of the average wage variable from the first-stage regression.

Measured labor-productivity differences across domestically owned plants could be affected by differences across industries in average hours worked. Since data on total paid man-hours are available only for production and related workers, the ratio of total man-hours paid for production and related workers divided by the total number of production and related workers in 1972 for domestically owned plants (M_i) was assumed to reflect the average hours worked by non-production workers and, therefore, by all employees in an industry.

Differences in labor productivity across manufacturing plants can conceptually be related to differences in economies of scale, which may, in turn, be plant- and/or product-specific. Plant-scale economies include those resulting from indivisibilities, increased specialization, and so on. Product-specific economies relate to length of production run, total planned output, and the rate of output per unit of time. In the absence of engineering cost estimates for our sample industries, an imputed measure of plant-scale economies must suffice. For countries with small domestic markets, such as Canada, estimates of minimum efficient scale (MES) plants are ordinarily derived from U.S. experience. Thus estimates of MES plants for our sample of Canadian industries were obtained by calculating the average size of the largest plants accounting for 50 percent of value added in comparably defined U.S. industries in 1972. The extent to which the "typical" domestically owned Canadian plant captured available plant-scale economies (E_i) was, in turn, measured as the ratio of the average value added in domestically owned plants in 1972 to our MES estimate.[1]

The absence of direct measures of product-scale economies imposes the need to construct an acceptable statistical proxy. The model of the protected oligopoly developed by Eastman and Stykolt[2] and supported by Bloch's[3] empirical results posits that excessive product diversification is characteristic of concentrated industries that enjoy significant levels of import protection. Hence product-scale economies attained by domestically owned plants were specified as an interaction variable (I_i) between the estimated nominal tariff rate for the industry in 1963 and a Herfindahl concentration measure based upon value of shipments for the industry in 1965. More specifically, the Herfindahl measure was multiplied by one if the industry's nominal tariff rate was above the median rate for all sample industries; otherwise, it was multiplied by zero.

To the extent that foreign direct investment provides "spillover" benefits to domestically owned factors of production, one would anticipate observing a positive relationship between labor productivity in domestically owned plants and some measure of foreign ownership in an industry. The precise form of the relationship is not obvious, however, on an *a priori* basis. Thus several alternative measures

---

[1] Expressed in Canadian dollars, using the average exchange rate for 1972.

[2] H. C. Eastman and S. Stykolt, *The Tariff and Competition in Canada* (Toronto: MacMillan, 1967).

[3] H. Bloch, "Prices, Costs and Profits in Canadian Manufacturing: The Influence of Tariffs and Concentration," *Canadian Journal of Economics* 4 (November, 1974): 594-610.

were employed. One proxy for the spillover benefits provided by foreign direct investment was the ratio of value added produced in foreign-owned plants to total industry value added in 1972 (F_{1i}). Another measured the external benefits of foreign direct investment as a binary variable (F_{2i}), taking a value of one if the share of industry value added produced in foreign-owned plants exceeded 50 percent in 1972 and taking a zero value otherwise. A third related labor productivity in domestically owned plants to value added by foreign-owned plants per employee in domestically owned plants in the ith industry for 1972 (F_{3i}).

Alternative linear specifications of the basic productivity equation were estimated. The equations reported below are for a sample of 61 industries. Note that the interaction variable I_i is not reported, as it was statistically insignificant in all equations. Furthermore, since there was little difference between equations employing either the L_{1i} or L_{3i} specification of labor quality, we report results only for the latter specification. A t statistic is shown in parentheses below each co-efficient; $\bar{R}^2$ is the adjusted overall co-efficient of determination.

1. $V_i = -6.626 + .139K_i + .655L_{3i} + 5.622M_i + 4.798E_i + .013F_{3i}$
$$\qquad\qquad\quad (4.74) \quad\ (1.72) \quad\ \ (1.19) \quad\quad (2.23) \quad\ (1.95)$$
$\bar{R}^2 = .658$

2. $V_i = -8.947 + .139K_i + .633L_{3i} + 6.348M_i + 5.339E_i + .026F_{1i}$
$$\qquad\qquad\quad (4.71) \quad\ (1.65) \quad\ \ (1.34) \quad\quad (2.33) \quad\ (1.85)$$
$\bar{R}^2 = .656$

The important point to note in this context is that both foreign ownership variables are statistically significant at the .05 level, which affords some evidence that foreign ownership provides spillover productivity benefits. Some notion of the relative importance of these benefits can be gathered by calculating mean elasticity co-efficients for the foreign ownership variables and comparing them to similar co-efficients calculated for the K_i and E_i variables in the above equations. The results, summarized in Table C.1, indicate that the productivity effects of foreign investment spillovers are modest in comparison to the productivity effects of capital deepening — that is, increasing K_i. They are somewhat smaller than the productivity effects of increasing average plant size — that is, increasing E_i.

It might be argued that the productivity effects of foreign ownership estimated above are to some extent spurious, in that they may reflect the fact that foreigners tend to invest in industries enjoying above-average rates of exogenous technological change. While this concern is potentially appropriate, the bulk of our sample industries cannot be considered to enjoy above-average rates of exogenous

TABLE C.1

Estimated Elasticity Co-efficients

Equation	$\dfrac{dV_i}{dK_i} \cdot \dfrac{\overline{K}_i}{\overline{V}_i}$	$\dfrac{dV_i}{dE_i} \cdot \dfrac{\overline{E}_i}{\overline{V}_i}$	$\dfrac{dV_i}{dF_{1i}} \cdot \dfrac{\overline{F}_{1i}}{\overline{V}_i}$	$\dfrac{dV_i}{dF_{3i}} \cdot \dfrac{\overline{F}_{3i}}{\overline{V}_i}$
1	.1631	.0489		.0335
2	.1627	.0546	.0506	

technological change. Specifically, about 50 percent of the sample is made up of firms in the food-products, textile and clothing, wood- and paper-products, and non-metallic-minerals industries. Another 17 percent are in primary- and fabricated-metals industries.

II

CANADA'S FOREIGN INVESTMENT REVIEW ACT: AN ECONOMIC APPRAISAL

1

Introduction

On April 9, 1974, the provisions under Canada's Foreign Investment Review Act (henceforth the Act) dealing with takeovers of Canadian businesses came into effect. The Minister of Industry, Trade and Commerce was designated as the minister responsible for the administration of the Act, and the Foreign Investment Review Agency (FIRA) was established to advise and assist the minister. The minister, in turn, reports to Cabinet, which has ultimate responsibility for the decision in any particular case. The takeover provisions of the Act require prior review and approval of acquisitions of control of Canadian businesses with gross assets of $250,000 or more or gross revenues of $3 million or more by "non-eligible persons."[1] The second phase of the Act — covering the establishment of new Canadian businesses by non-eligible persons who do not already have an existing business in Canada, as well as the establishment by non-eligible persons of new Canadian businesses that are not related to businesses they are already carrying on in Canada — came into effect on October 15, 1975.[2]

Tables 1 and 2 provide an overview of FIRA's activities under the two sections of the Act. Specifically, Table 1 reports a summary of FIRA's reviewable acquisition cases, and Table 2 reports a summary of FIRA's reviewable new-business cases, through 1977. As shown, the majority of resolved applications reviewed by FIRA for either acquisitions or new-business investment were approved. As might be expected, the bulk of reviewable applications were from U.S. investors.[3]

---

[1] A description of the takeover provisions of the Act is contained in Foreign Investment Review Agency (FIRA), *Foreign Investment Review Act Annual Report*, 1974/75 (Ottawa, 1975). New acquisition regulations permit the filing of notice of a proposed acquisition in a much abbreviated form where the Canadian business being acquired has gross assets of less than $2 million and fewer than one hundred employees. A "non-eligible person" is a foreign individual, corporation, or government or a group containing foreign members.

[2] A description of the overall review process is provided in FIRA, *Foreign Investment Review Act Annual Report*, 1975/76 (Ottawa, 1976).

[3] It can be determined from the data in Tables 1 and 2 that observed differences across countries in the percentage of resolved cases receiving approval are primarily due to chance. Furthermore, no significant difference exists between the proportion

58

TABLE 1

Summary of FIRA Reviewable Acquisition Cases and Percentage
of Resolved Cases Allowed, April 9, 1974-December 30, 1977

Origin of Acquirers	Reviewable Cases	Percentage of Resolved Cases Allowed
United States	457	80
United Kingdom	99	83
Other European	117	69
Other countries	27	63
All countries	700	78

Source: Author's calculations from Foreign Investment Review Agency, *Foreign Investment Review* 1, No. 3 (1978): 26-27.

TABLE 2

Summary of FIRA Reviewable New-Business Cases
and Percentage of Resolved Cases Allowed,
October 15, 1975-December 30, 1977

Origin of Acquirers	Reviewable Cases	Percentage of Resolved Cases Allowed
United States	278	83
United Kingdom	52	87
Other European	149	88
Other countries	51	83
All countries	530	85

Source: See Table 1.

Table 3 reports the average asset sizes of acquired companies whose acquisitions by non-eligible investors were reviewable by FIRA. Quite clearly, the majority of reviewable foreign acquisitions (through the end of 1978) involved relatively small companies.[4] Specifically, well over 80 percent of the acquisition cases involved acquirees with less than $5 million in assets. Data presented in Table 4 indicate that approximately 50 percent of the reviewable acquisition cases in the first three years were in the manufaturing sector. Approximately 22 percent were in wholesale and retail trade. In short, the majority of reviewable acquisition cases have involved relatively small Canadian companies in a few specific industrial sectors and have been accorded approval by FIRA.

of applications for acquisitions that were approved and the proportion of applications for new businesses that were approved.

[4] Data drawn from FIRA's annual reports correspond to that agency's fiscal year, which ends March 31. Data in Tables 3 to 5, therefore, are not directly comparable to those in Tables 1 and 2.

TABLE 3

Average Assets of Acquirees, 1974/75-76/77[a]

Type of Acquiree	Number of Cases			Average Assets of Acquirees		
	1974/75	1975/76	1976/77	1974/75	1975/76	1976/77
				(thousand dollars)		
Canadian-controlled:						
Private	79	61	70	3,088	3,376	3,564
Public	18	8		17,008	4,200	
Foreign-controlled:						
Private	43	66	116	7,212	4,409	7,267
Public	10	9		11,051	15,552	
All:						
Private	122	127	186	4,542	3,912	5,877
Public	28	17		14,880	10,210	

[a]For fiscal years ending March 31.

Source: FIRA, *Foreign Investment Review Act Annual Report* (Ottawa, various issues).

TABLE 4

Reviewable Acquisition Cases, by Industry Sector, 1974/75-76/77[a]

Industry Sector	Number of Cases		
	1974/75	1975/76	1976/77
Mines, mineral fuels, and incidental services	17	14	10
Other primary	5	2	3
Manufacturing	65	75	98
Construction	2	4	4
Transportation, communication, and other utilities	8	5	5
Wholesale and retail trade	31	29	47
Finance, insurance, and real estate	16	10	9
Community, business, and personal services	6	5	10
	150	144	186

[a]For fiscal years ending March 31.

Source: See Table 3.

The Act represents one outcome of the extended public scrutiny and debate of the issue of foreign ownership in Canada. It can be fairly stated that reaction to the Act and to FIRA's activities has been quite mixed. FIRA officials contend that the Act has been a source of significant net benefits for Canadians; however, a number of investigators support the contention of many Canadian "nationalists" that the administration of the Act has had no significant impact on foreign direct investment in Canada.[5] Louis A. Calvet argues that the Act has resulted in foreign investors' altering their proposals in line with screening criteria and that, to that extent, it can be credited with positive achievements; however, Calvet is not able to conclude that the alterations have been unambiguously good for Canada.[6] To complete the spectrum of opinion, some observers have argued that FIRA should be scuttled in order to encourage foreign capital formation in Canada; others claim that FIRA restricts owners of small Canadian businesses from selling their businesses at full capitalized values.[7]

In light of the major controversy that continues to surround FIRA and the potential importance of FIRA's activities to the Canadian economy, the relative dearth of scholarly enquiries into the economic impact of the Act is disturbing.[8] Indeed, specific criticisms and analyses of FIRA have focused largely on the absence of well-defined trade-offs among the various screening criteria[9] or on alleged weaknesses in FIRA's operating procedures.[10] Conspicuously absent is any overall economic consideration of the basic premises underlying the Act or any attempt to analyze systematically the available evidence of FIRA's impact on foreign investment.

---

[5] See, for example, Talaat Abdel-Malek and Asit Sarkar, "An Analysis of the Effects of Phase II Guidelines of the Foreign Investment Review Act," *Canadian Public Policy* 3, No. 1 (Winter, 1977): 36-49; Charles J. McMillan, "The Regulation of Foreign Investment in Canada: Experience and Prospects," mimeographed, York University, Toronto, 1977; and Alan Rugman, "The Regulation of Foreign Investment in Canada," *Journal of World Trade Law* 11 (September-October, 1977): 322-33.

[6] Louis A. Calvet, *Canadian Controls of Foreign Business Entry: Present Form and Future Prospects*, Working Paper 959-77 (Cambridge, Mass.: Alfred P. Sloan School of Management, Massachusetts Institute of Technology, 1977).

[7] See, for example, the statement by T. S. Ripley in *Globe and Mail* (Toronto), May 19, 1976. More recently, it was reported that Prime Minister Trudeau, in private talks with a provincial premier, raised the possibility of temporarily suspending FIRA. Trudeau was reportedly concerned with the possibility that foreign investors feel unwelcome in Canada. (See David Blaikie, "Trudeau May Suspend FIRA," *Toronto Star*, November 15, 1977.)

[8] FIRA is trying to stimulate greater research into issues surrounding the Act by, among other things, publishing a magazine dealing with the review process.

[9] An example of such criticism is found in Lawrence A. Skeoch and Bruce McDonald, *Dynamic Change and Accountability in a Canadian Market Economy* (Ottawa: Department of Consumer and Corporate Affairs, 1976).

[10] Some recent criticism has focused on FIRA's apparent unwillingness or inability to enforce commitments undertaken by foreign firms. One such case involved British-owned Marks and Spencer Ltd. (See Wayne Chevaldayoff, "Secrecy Cloaks FIRA's Easing of Takeover Rules," *Globe and Mail* [Toronto], October 4, 1977.) It should be noted that FIRA is expected to investigate significant departures by foreign investors from the original terms of agreement. For a recent critical review of FIRA, see A. E. Safarian, "Presidential Address: Policy on Multinational Enterprises in Developed Countries," *Canadian Journal of Economics* 11, No. 4 (November, 1978): 641-56.

This monograph represents an attempt to bring the public-policy debate surrounding FIRA into sharper focus by providing a structured consideration of the specific conditions under which FIRA (or any similar mechanism for screening foreign investment) could be expected to provide net benefits to the Canadian economy. As a corollary, a structured consideration of the potential distributional consequences of FIRA's activities is also provided. The study considers, as a related issue, the conditions under which the bilateral impacts of FIRA coincide with domestic impacts — that is, does promoting the domestic net benefits of U.S. foreign direct investment in Canada necessarily reduce the benefits of such investment realized by Americans?[11] An effort is made to evaluate empirically the important hypotheses underlying the conceptual framework developed in the monograph, although it must be acknowledged that the empirical analysis — including a case study of the appliance industry — is far from comprehensive or conclusive. This disclaimer notwithstanding, the study does suggest that concern on the part of some Canadians about the net benefits of FIRA is appropriate. More specifically, a creditable, if not definitive, conceptual and empirical case can be made that the Act imposes net economic costs on Canadians generally and, possibly, upon foreign investors as well. Potentially important redistributional effects of FIRA's activities can also be identified.

The next chapter outlines quite briefly the major events leading up to the passage of the Act. Such a review helps to identify the major governmental arguments underlying the ostensible premise of the Act — that is, that the goal of achieving an efficient and competitive economy can be promoted by screening incoming foreign direct investment. This review also provides a historical background against which the current policy climate toward foreign ownership in Canada can be evaluated.

---

[11]In more technical terms, the monograph explicitly identifies the set of conditions under which the bilateral direct investment process is either a "zero-sum" or a "positive-sum" game.

2

Background to the Act[1]

Although concern about foreign investment dates back to Confederation, the roots of the foreign ownership debate in Canada probably date most specifically from the Royal Commission on Canada's Economic Prospects, which issued its report in 1957.[2] While the Commission, headed by Walter Gordon, identified the major areas in which foreign ownership was dominant and expressed strong concern about the potential influence wielded by large foreign companies in Canada, no significant legislative action followed directly from its report.

In 1967 the federal government established a task force, headed by Professor Melville Watkins, to undertake a major investigation of the causes and consequences of foreign investment in Canada. The task force published its findings and recommendations in 1968.[3] Its report included a recommendation to create a government agency to handle surveillance of multinational companies operating in Canada. The Liberal government did not act immediately upon any of the recommendations in the Watkins Report, although in 1970 a parliamentary standing committee, chaired by Ian Wahn, was established to examine Canadian-U.S. relations, including U.S. investment in Canada. The Wahn Committee, while reinforcing the thrust of the Watkins Report's recommendations, went somewhat further in recommending, among other things, that all foreign-owned firms in Canada should, over a reasonable period of time, allow for at least 51 percent of their voting shares to be owned by Canadian citizens.[4]

The federal government initiated the most comprehensive study of the issue of foreign ownership in Canada in 1970, when it formed

---

[1] A more comprehensive review of events leading up to the publication of the Gray Report is found in Charles McMillan, "After the Gray Report: The Tortuous Evolution of Foreign Investment Policy," *McGill Law Journal* 20, No. 2 (1974): 1-27.
[2] *Final Report of the Royal Commission on Canada's Economic Prospects* (Gordon Report) (Ottawa: Queen's Printer, 1957).
[3] Task Force on the Structure of Canadian Industry, *Foreign Ownership and the Structure of Canadian Industry* (Watkins Report) (Ottawa: Queen's Printer, 1968).
[4] *Report of the House of Commons Standing Committee on External Affairs and National Defence* (Ottawa: Queen's Printer, 1970).

a task force reporting to the Hon. Herb Gray, M.P. The theoretical underpinnings of the Gray Report's recommendations, released in 1972, will be examined in a later section. At this point we merely note the report's major conclusion, which established the government's rationale for the Act — that a review process for certain types of foreign direct investment would increase the net benefits of such investment realized by Canadians.[5]

While the Gray Report provides a general discussion of areas in which net benefits from foreign direct investment might be increased, the Act itself contains specific criteria for evaluating whether a proposed acquisition or the proposed establishment of a new enterprise by a non-eligible person is likely to be of significant benefit to Canada. The criteria include:[6]

- The effects on the level and nature of economic activity in Canada, including the effects on employment; on resource processing; on the utilization of Canadian parts, components, and services; and on exports.

- The degree and the significance of participation by Canadians in the business enterprise and in the industry sector to which the enterprise belongs.

- The effects on productivity, industrial efficiency, technological development, innovation, and product variety.

- The effects on competition within any industry or among industries in Canada.

- Compatibility with national industrial and economic policies, taking into consideration industrial- and economic-policy objectives enunciated by a province likely to be significantly affected by the proposed investment.

The Act might be criticized for not providing priority orderings for these various criteria; however, the central issue posed by the Gray Report's major recommendation is whether FIRA can increase the benefits of the direct investment process over and above any additional costs imposed by the review procedure. A related concern is how any additional benefits and/or costs attendant upon FIRA's activities are distributed within the domestic economy. While FIRA claims it has produced substantial benefits for Canada, such claims cannot be accepted at face value, both because of the limited available information relating to the disposition of reviewed cases and because the impact of FIRA's decisions is likely to extend beyond the

---

[5] *Foreign Direct Investment in Canada* (Gray Report) (Ottawa: Government of Canada, 1972).

[6] FIRA, *Foreign Investment Review Act Annual Report,* 1975/76 (Ottawa, 1976), p. 11.

individual cases considered.[7] Indeed, any evaluation of FIRA should be made within a "general equilibrium" framework that takes into account all major direct and indirect effects of FIRA's activities. We turn now to the development of such a framework.

---

[7] For example, FIRA claims that the benefits of its activities in fiscal year 1974/75 included some seven thousand new jobs as well as improvements in efficiency and technology (see FIRA, *Foreign Investment Review Act Annual Report*, 1974/75 [Ottawa, 1975], p. 1).

3

A General Framework for Evaluating FIRA's Economic Effects

FIRA's potential effects are quite broad and encompass issues difficult to quantify, such as enhanced political sovereignty. Rather than attempting to grapple with intractable conceptual and empirical difficulties, this investigation is limited to a single measure of domestic welfare — real incomes of domestically owned factors of production. More specifically, this chapter seeks to establish the precise conditions under which FIRA's review procedure could be expected to increase (or decrease) real incomes of domestically owned factors of production. By focusing upon FIRA's potential pecuniary effects, we will have a useful benchmark against which any non-pecuniary benefits of increased Canadian ownership of domestic assets can be assessed.

It is convenient, and not overly restrictive, to focus the analysis on foreign takeover activity — that is, on the first phase of the Act. As a justification for adopting this focus, one need only recognize that a foreign takeover is equivalent to, albeit sometimes cheaper than, purchasing separately all the various assets sought in a domestic aquisition. While foreigners will frequently have a preference between purchasing Canadian-owned assets already embodied in an existing firm — for example, buying an existing plant from a domestic owner — and purchasing disembodied assets — for example, contracting for the building of a new plant in Canada — the motives for their choices are not of primary concern, since the conditions under which FIRA can be expected to increase the real incomes of Canadians are identical for all forms of foreign direct investment.[1]

Imperfectly Competitive Markets and Takeover "Rents"

The starting point for any consideration of FIRA's activities is the hypothesis that some degree of imperfection in input and/or product markets exists in Canada, which makes possible the entry and

---

[1] The literature on the determinants of merger activity provides an extensive discussion of the advantages of internal versus external expansion (see, for example, Peter O. Steiner, *Mergers: Motives, Effects, Policies* [Ann Arbor: University of Michigan Press, 1975]).

perpetuation of foreign investments that reduce the economic welfare of Canadians. Only to the extent that this hypothesis is valid will FIRA be able to improve the economic benefits for Canada from the direct investment. That is, if all markets in Canada, including the market for corporate acquisitions, were efficient and competitive, the foreign takeover of domestically owned firms (or of other foreign-owned firms) would provide no opportunity for FIRA to increase the net domestic economic benefits of the takeover.[2]

The latter point can be expanded. If any foreign firm is to purchase a firm operating in Canada (whether domestically owned or foreign-owned), it must be able and willing to outbid all domestically owned firms for the assets in question. If a foreign firm can outbid domestically owned firms, and if the required price differential is less than the maximum differential the foreign firm would be willing to pay (to outbid potential domestic buyers), foreign firms can be said to realize "rents" on domestic acquisitions — that is, the price of the acquisition to the foreigner can be increased without necessarily discouraging the acquisition from taking place. Whether forcing a foreign acquirer to pay a higher price (when buying a business in Canada) increases or decreases the economic welfare of Canadians therefore depends upon a number of factors, including the source of the foreign acquirer's higher expected rate of return on domestic acquisitions and, in some cases, the efficiency of the "market" for corporate acquisitions in Canada. The above-mentioned hypothesis can be developed by examining several suggested reasons why foreign firms might undertake investments having potentially adverse economic consequences for Canada and/or gain rents by acquiring assets in Canada.

Power in Product Markets

It has been argued that the possession of special marketing and technological resources provides foreign firms with both potential efficiency advantages and a source of market power in Canadian product markets. It is further argued that marketing and/or technological expertise is frequently transferable from the parent company to a subsidiary at a relatively low cost, particularly if the parent company has "surplus" resources or is operating below its full capacity.[3] The low-cost transferability of market power allegedly

---

[2] It should be noted explicitly that FIRA also reviews foreign takeovers of foreign-owned firms, although there is some basis for arguing that domestic acquisitions are scrutinized more closely than foreign acquisitions. One piece of evidence is that the acceptance rate for ownership transfers of foreign-controlled companies is higher than that of large domestically owned companies. The respective rates were 70 percent and 56 percent in 1975/76. (See FIRA, *Foreign Investment Review Act Annual Report*, 1975/76 [Ottawa, 1976], p. 39.)

[3] See Bernard Wolf, "Industrial Diversification and Internationalization: Some Empirical Evidence," *Journal of Industrial Economics* 26, No. 2 (December, 1977): 177-91.

enables foreign firms to earn higher rates of return (over and above any higher returns reflecting greater efficiency) than Canadian-owned firms and, therefore, to outbid Canadian-owned firms on purchases of domestic assets. If the higher anticipated rate of return to the successful foreign acquirer primarily reflects expected monopoly profits (or monopoly "rents") extracted ultimately from domestic consumers, it can be argued that the acquisition should be prevented or, equivalently, that the foreign acquirer should be required to act as a competitive producer as a condition of purchase. For example, the foreign firm might be required, as a condition of purchase, to commit itself to produce a greater volume of output and to hire a larger number of workers than it otherwise would. At the extreme, the foreign firm would be required to produce the "competitive" rate of output.[4]

Setting aside considerations of how FIRA — or, indeed, any other agency — might succeed in transforming an anti-competitive merger to one having benign effects upon competition,[5] the relevance of the above-cited monopoly argument can be questioned on a number of grounds. The argument is largely predicated on the observation that foreign ownership levels are high in industries with high industrial concentration ratios — that is, in industries where a few firms produce the bulk of industry output. However, industrial concentration is, by itself, a very inexact index of the degree of competition in an industry. Indeed, it might be argued that foreign acquisitions in concentrated industries (that is, those dominated by a relatively few firms) actually increase effective competition by destabilizing existing market shares and established firms' positions.[6] Furthermore, the relationship between foreign ownership and concentration might largely reflect the facts that foreign firms are particularly efficient managers of larger domestic subsidiaries and that large average firm size and industrial concentration are positively related.[7]

---

[4] Note that this would be tantamount to requiring the foreign firm to pay a higher effective price for the acquisition. Quite clearly, this is a difficult policy to implement in practice, since the "competitive" rate of output is not observable. Furthermore, the policy would have the associated effect of increasing the percentage of output produced by foreign-owned firms. However, the key point is that, if foreigners earn monopoly "rents" from domestic acquisitions, FIRA could presumably impose costly requirements on the foreign acquirer without discouraging takeovers.

[5] No effort is made here to enter into a consideration of whether domestic competition legislation or the Act is the more appropriate device for screening foreign takeovers to gain monopoly positions in domestic markets. A closely related concern is the notion that the acquisition of a domestic company may enable a foreign firm to preserve a monopoly position in Canada.

[6] Examples of how international mergers have destabilized existing "collusive" practices in oligopolistic industries are provided in Jack Behrman, *National Interests and the Multinational Enterprise* (Englewood Cliffs, N.J.: Prentice-Hall, 1970).

[7] A related notion is that intrafirm exchange rather than arm's-length exchange of goods and services economizes on transactions costs in concentrated industries. This notion is developed in Steven Globerman, "Canada-U.S. Economic Linkages

The potential for foreign-owned firms to realize monopoly profits associated with the acquisition of domestic assets is obviously difficult to quantify. Indirect evidence, however, suggests that international competition among multinational firms increased over the postwar period. More specifically, the degree of seller concentration in world markets has shown a definite tendency to decline in the postwar period. For example, among the world's largest firms the percentage of worldwide sales accounted for by U.S. firms fell from roughly 68 percent in 1962 to approximately 59 percent in 1972. A similar decline in the U.S. share occurred for worldwide sales of the 25, 50, and 100 largest companies. This decline has resulted primarily from the competition of Japanese, German, and other companies that have successfully penetrated the markets of U.S. firms.[8]

More direct evidence calling into question the notion that foreign investors expect to realize monopoly "rents" on corporate acquisitions in Canada is provided by the observation that the after-tax rate of return on domestic (that is, U.S.) capital investment exceeded the after-tax rate of return on U.S. direct investment in Canada over the period 1960-69.[9] In short, there is some reason to argue that most foreign acquisitions reviewed by FIRA are unlikely to reduce competition levels in Canadian industries or to provide foreign investors with significant monopoly profits.

Discount-Rate Differentials

A foreign purchaser may be able to outbid potential Canadian buyers for a domestically owned asset if foreign investors, for one reason or another, have lower costs of capital than domestic investors.[10] In this regard, it has been suggested that Canadian owners are generally more risk-averse and more pessimistic about business conditions than their U.S. counterparts.[11] Thus Canadians may assign a lower present value to expected future earnings from a domestic business than do foreigners.

If, in fact, Canadian investors are "excessively" risk-averse — or systematically underestimate, for whatever reason, the value of

---

Through the Direct Investment Process," mimeographed, York University, Toronto, 1978.

[8] This evidence is presented and discussed in Robert G. Hawkins, "Are Multinational Corporations Depriving the United States of Its Economic Diversity and Independence?," in Carl H. Madden, ed., *The Case for the Multinational Corporation* (New York: Praeger, 1977).

[9] See Herbert Grubel, "Taxation and the Rates of Return from Some U.S. Asset Holdings Abroad, 1960-69," *Journal of Political Economy* 82, No. 3 (May-June, 1974): 469-89.

[10] The lower the cost of capital used to discount expected net earnings, the higher the present value of a capital asset.

[11] Some of the differences in perceived attitudes toward risk may be due to the real risk-spreading advantages that the international diversification of investment provides the multinational firm. This question is examined in Robert M. Dunn, Jr., *The*

domestic assets — foreign investors may realize "rents" on acquisitions of domestic assets. One might then rationalize FIRA's review process on the grounds that it could "correct" the evaluations of Canadian investors and/or effectively force foreign acquirers to pay more for specific acquisitions by requiring them to undertake certain commitments that they would not otherwise undertake.[12] In principle, therefore, FIRA might be able to reduce, or eliminate, any rents earned by foreign acquirers by intervening in the takeover process.

It should be noted that, even if Canadians "undervalue" domestic assets, competitive bidding among foreign firms might force the selling prices of these assets to equal their "true" present values.[13] A prevalent view, mentioned in the Gray Report and elsewhere, is that foreigners can act as monopsonistic purchasers of domestically owned assets. Consequently, competitive bidding for Canadian-owned businesses rarely takes place. Unfortunately, little direct evidence is available on the question of whether foreign firms generally act as competitive or monopsonistic buyers of Canadian assets. The larger average firm size of foreign firms is frequently offered as a rationale for believing that foreigners can obtain Canadian businesses at bargain prices. However, some evidence suggests that larger firms do not necessarily acquire domestic companies at lower prices than do smaller firms. Martin found that, for a sample of Canadian acquisitions, the average transaction involved a purchase premium of $1.3 million, or 47 percent, above the book value of net assets acquired. This premium was proportionally greatest (84 percent) for acquiring companies of the largest size.[14]

The fact that foreign ownership is high in concentrated industries is also pointed to as evidence that competitive bidding among foreign firms for domestic assets ordinarily does not take place. It should be noted in this regard that, if collusion among potential acquirers does not exist, competitive bidding could arise even in the presence of a fairly small number of potential buyers. Furthermore,

---

Canada-U.S. Capital Market: Intermediation, Integration, and Policy Independence, Canada-U.S. Prospects series (Montreal and Washington, D.C.: C. D. Howe Research Institute and National Planning Association, 1978).

[12] For example, a foreign acquirer might be required to do more R & D in Canada and to purchase less R & D from its parent. Note that the "undervaluation" hypothesis would not necessarily support the screening of foreign takeovers of foreign-owned firms. Moreover, the process of monitoring implied by advance commitments raises problems that may not be at all trivial. A closely related notion is that FIRA might be able to price-discriminate more effectively than sellers of domestic assets, thereby capturing the "rent," or consumer surplus, realized on intramarginal purchases of domestic assets by foreigners.

[13] It is virtually impossible to define "true" present value, but (in this case) it can be thought of as the net earnings of the asset discounted over time by the social discount rate.

[14] See Samuel A. Martin, Stanley W. Laiken, and Douglas F. Haslam, *Business Combinations in the 60's: A Canadian Profile* (Toronto: Canadian Institute of Chartered Accountants, 1969).

acquisition data imply that sellers of domestic assets may confront a broader range of potential buyers than is suggested by gross industry concentration ratios. Over the period 1945-61, for example, about 75 percent of international firms acquiring domestic companies purchased one company, or at most two. Over the period 1972-74 the percentage of foreign acquirers making more than one acquisition was consistently below 10 percent.[15] Thus most foreign firms do not undertake multiple acquisitions of domestic companies; this belies the notion that Canadian firms typically confront only a very few potential buyers of their assets. In summary, even if domestic investors initially "undervalue" domestic assets, foreign firms may, on average, realize no "rents" on domestic acquisitions if the corporate-acquisition market in Canada is reasonably competitive and efficient. Put alternatively, if competitive bidding among potential acquirers ordinarily forces foreign firms to pay up to their maximum prices in order to acquire domestic assets, FIRA's review process cannot extract higher effective prices without discouraging the acquisitions from taking place.

Provincial Competition for Foreign Investment

A plausible argument for the existence of takeover "rents" is that competition among provincial governments for foreign direct investment enables foreigners to acquire domestic assets at lower prices than they would otherwise pay.[16] For example, local or regional development grants or tax incentives may be extended to foreign firms, thereby increasing the return earned by the foreign investor above that required to encourage an investment to be made. Calvet suggests that one of the principal missions of FIRA, in the eyes of its officials, is to unite the provinces under the federal authority and thereby to avoid competition in granting concessions and inducements to foreign investors.[17]

Several caveats are relevant in evaluating the provincial competition argument. One is that competition among foreign firms for Canadian government grants and tax assistance (at all levels of government) may ensure that any subsidies are "passed through" to domestic factors of production. For example, if two or more foreign firms are willing to undertake an investment without government aid, the prospect of a financial subsidy might encourage the firms to offer higher prices for the assets in question or to agree to undertake

---

[15] A full discussion of these data is provided in Steven Globerman, *Mergers and Acquisitions in Canada* (Ottawa: Supply and Services Canada, 1977).

[16] This situation might arise if provincial governments wanted to encourage an expansion of economic activity in industries where there were a very limited number of potential domestic investors.

[17] See Louis A. Calvet, *Canadian Controls of Foreign Business Entry: Present Form and Future Prospects*, Working Paper 959-77 (Cambridge, Mass.: Alfred P. Sloan School of Management, Massachusetts Institute of Technology, 1977), p. 35.

TABLE 5

Reviewable Acquisition Cases, 1974/75-76/77[a]

Province	Number of Cases			Assets of Acquirees		
	1974/75	1975/76	1976/77	1974/75	1975/76	1976/77
				(thousand dollars)		
Atlantic provinces	5	6	3	26,059	27,814	4,388
Quebec	39	27	38	222,201	163,795	353,224
Ontario	59	71	105	430,363	266,344	465,880
Western provinces:						
Manitoba	5	5	7	68,605	80,050	22,405
Saskatchewan	2	2	1			
Alberta	23	17	20	151,129	88,708	129,768
British Columbia	17	16	12	72,370	43,730	117,002
	150	144	186	970,727	670,441	1,092,667

[a]Note that acquirees are classified by province of principal location.

Source: See Table 3.

certain activities they otherwise would not (for example, offer general manpower-training programs) in order to receive a favorable judgment from the granting authority.

Another caveat is that the bulk of foreign acquisitions of particular types are located in specific provinces. Table 5 provides a regional breakdown of the location of acquirees in reviewable acquisition cases. It can be seen that the bulk of acquisitions, by number and by assets, involve companies located in Quebec, Ontario, and Alberta. Acquisitions cross-classified by industry and by region are unavailable; however, one can reasonably argue that many acquisitions in Alberta involve natural resource assets not located in Quebec and Ontario. Furthermore, differences in industry mix in Quebec and Ontario raise the possibility that many foreign direct investments pose no problems of government competition among Canada's main manufacturing provinces.[18] Thus, while the potential for political competition for foreign direct investment undoubtedly exists in some cases, it may not be particularly relevant in the majority of foreign acquisitions of domestic assets.

[18]Noteworthy differences include the fact that the automotive industry and such "high-technology" industries as aerospace firms and producers of electronic equipment are primarily located in Ontario, while textile and apparel firms are largely located in Quebec. It is not obvious what effect the election of the Parti Québécois will have on interprovincial competition. On the surface, it would appear to reduce Ontario's need to offer relocation concessions to foreign firms. However, the recent example of the Ontario and Quebec governments' "lobbying" for a General Motors aluminum die-casting plant is a significant exception to this statement (see *Globe and Mail* [Toronto], June 17, 1978).

Efficiency Motives

In the preceding sections a number of general explanations of foreign acquisitions were considered and rejected. These explanations implied that foreign acquirers ordinarily earn significant "rents" on acquired assets and/or receive returns that at least partly reflect substantial monopoly profits. Having argued that these explanations do not appear to have *general* validity, it is appropriate to seek an alternative general explanation of foreign acquisitions and to consider how, assuming that the explanation has validity, FIRA might then improve the economic benefits from foreign acquisitions.

A plausible general interpretation of why foreign buyers can outbid Canadian firms for specific domestic assets is that foreign firms can utilize the purchased assets more productively than can potential Canadian buyers. A number of factors can be suggested as contributing to this situation. One is the frequently cited advantage that foreign firms have in adopting and utilizing new technology. More specifically, many observers argue that it is easier and less costly to transfer technology within the multinational corporation than among separately owned firms. The presumably easier access that foreign subsidiaries have to managerial expertise is another factor. A third is the possibility that foreign subsidiaries can obtain quantity discounts on inputs by "tying on" to parent purchases. These discounts, in turn, might reflect real cost savings associated with economies of scale.[19]

If superior efficiency is the underlying motive for most foreign acquisitions of domestic assets (and if foreigners ordinarily pay up to their maximum price for domestic assets, as suggested above), it is not likely that Canada's economic interests would be served by discouraging such acquisitions. Indeed, if the derived or "spillover" effects of foreign acquisitions include lower prices for consumers and/or increased productivity in domestically owned firms, restrictions on foreign direct investment will impart net economic costs to the Canadian economy.[20]

The possibility does exist that FIRA might increase the benefits of such foreign acquisitions if the review process leads the foreign investor to be even more efficient than would be the case in the absence of the review. The Gray Report raises this possibility in suggesting that FIRA's screening procedure might alert foreign-owned firms to opportunities they would not ordinarily recognize. For example, foreign-owned firms may systematically overestimate costs of performing R & D in Canada and therefore "overcentralize"

---

[19]Some specific evidence bearing on the hypothesis that foreign-owned firms in Canada are generally more efficient than their domestically owned counterparts is provided in Globerman, "Canada-U.S. Economic Linkages," *op. cit.*

[20]*Ibid.* Globerman provides further discussion and empirical evidence on the existence of "spillover" efficiency benefits to foreign direct investment.

R & D performance in the parent company. Another possibility is that the requirement that the foreign investor increase Canadian management (and, possibly, ownership) in the venture might provide the foreigner with a better understanding of the economic and cultural environment and therefore make a contribution to improved efficiency and higher profits.[21]

The possibility that FIRA's review procedure will increase a foreign firm's anticipated benefits from purchasing domestic assets is unlikely, however, for a number of reasons. One is that it would clearly be in the best interest of any seller to inform all potential foreign buyers of the most efficient way to operate in the domestic economy. Another is that FIRA would be unlikely to have more information than a foreign acquirer about how to utilize purchased resources most efficiently in the Canadian economy. This presumption is reinforced by observing that FIRA must often go to outside experts for technical guidance and that FIRA ordinarily does not communicate with the selling company.[22]

---

[21] See Frank Swedlove, "The Joint Venture Alternative for Investing in Canada," *Foreign Investment Review* 1, No. 2 (Winter, 1977/78): 16.

[22] These observations are made in Calvet, *op. cit.* The fact that sellers of domestic assets are ordinarily more knowledgeable than FIRA about the value to the foreign purchaser of the assets acquired also makes it unlikely that FIRA can price-discriminate more successfully than domestic sellers on the intramarginal domestic assets purchased by foreigners.

4

An Overview of the Basic Issues

The preceding chapter presented the major arguments that have been advanced in support of FIRA's review procedure. The conclusion drawn was that the vast majority of foreign acquisitions are unlikely to reduce competition in domestic markets or provide significant economic "rents" to foreigners. If, in fact, foreigners ordinarily pay up to their maximum acquisition prices for domestic assets, any additional costs or burdens imposed by the review process will discourage some foreign acquisitions from taking place. Before turning to a consideration of the direct and indirect economic effects of reduced foreign acquisitions, some further attention will be given to the issue of how "costly" FIRA's screening process is to foreign firms.

One can certainly imagine the possibility that FIRA operates the review process in such an exceedingly flexible and careful way that commitments to demonstrate significant benefit are extracted only in those atypical situations where "rent" is indeed present in a foreign acquisition and/or where the acquisition clearly has anti-competitive consequences for the economy. However, given the realities of the review process, it would strain the limits of credulity to accept this interpretation. Being subject to time and resource constraints, FIRA operates — at best — in an environment of imperfect information; its decision processes are more likely characterized as following "rule-of-thumb" criteria — that is, applications that are broadly similar in nature tend to be accorded broadly similar treatment. Rule-of-thumb criteria are unlikely to provide precise decisions within any group of investment applications or, necessarily, across groups. More specifically, the need for FIRA to adopt broad-based criteria for evaluating foreign acquisitions makes it unlikely that it will be able to identify precisely those cases where significant "rents" are likely to be earned by foreign acquirers.

Another important consideration — and one frequently overlooked in evaluations of the Act — is that FIRA is essentially a political agency, with final accountability to Cabinet. Given its minimal public-reporting obligations (or opportunities), FIRA is susceptible to being used to foster political objectives or "special interests" rather than being employed strictly for improving the terms of

74

exchange for sales of domestic assets in Canada.[1] The recognition that FIRA is subject to real political constraints further reduces the likelihood that required commitments will precisely capture any "rents" associated with specific foreign takeovers.

Yet another reason for suggesting that the Act may, at least for borderline cases, raise the costs of specific acquisitions above their anticipated present values, and hence discourage the acquisitions from taking place, is that the costs of the review procedure itself may not be insignificant. Some observers have argued that a large portion of the costs associated with the review process were related to initial uncertainty surrounding the criteria FIRA would employ and that, with the passage of time, this uncertainty has been mitigated by experience. However, while uncertainty has probably been reduced, the applicant must now hire specialized legal counsel familiar with FIRA's procedures. It is unlikely that such expertise is obtainable at an insignificant cost. Furthermore, a substantial amount of executive time is often tied up by the application procedure.[2]

If one accepts the hypotheses that the review process increases the costs of undertaking foreign acquisitions and that significant "rents" are not ordinarily associated with foreign acquisitions of domestic assets, then the review process will encourage a decrease in the long-run supply of specific forms of foreign direct investment in Canada.[3] The economic implications of such a decrease are considered in the following section.

FIRA's Potential Direct and Indirect Effects on Aggregate Income

The full implications of a reduction in the supply of incoming direct investment are quite complex. The arguments presented in this section are kept at a relatively general level, but they reflect an extended and technical analysis performed by the author.[4]

General Costs

A reduced supply of foreign direct investment will result in foreigners' not only undertaking a smaller number of acquisitions but also paying a lower average price on all acquisitions made compared to the average price that would be paid in the absence of the

---

[1] The political constraints influencing FIRA's decision-making processes are considered in the case study presented in Chapter 6.
[2] Calvet reports that companies continue to complain about the time and cost involved in the application procedure (Louis A. Calvet, *Canadian Controls of Foreign Business Entry: Present Form and Future Prospects*, Working Paper 959-77 [Cambridge, Mass.: Alfred P. Sloan School of Management, Massachusetts Institute of Technology, 1977], p. 21).
[3] The extent of the decrease and the specific forms affected will depend, among other things, upon the nature of the demands FIRA makes upon particular investors. Empirical evidence bearing on this issue is considered in Chapter 5.
[4] This analysis is reported in Steven Globerman, "An Economic Analysis of the

review process. For acquisitions of domestically owned firms this process represents a loss of wealth for Canadian owners and, therefore, a cost of the review process to Canada.[5] The reduction in foreign acquisitions also imposes general costs upon Canadians to the extent that indirect or "spillover" efficiency benefits to consumers and to domestic factors of production accompany foreign acquisitions.[6]

Offsetting the above-mentioned losses to some extent are the commitments, extracted through the review process, for foreigners to undertake certain costly activities. The value of these commitments can be viewed, in essence, as the proceeds of a tax on capital imports. The magnitude of the proceeds will depend largely upon the substitutability existing between reviewable forms of foreign direct investment and other vehicles for exploiting a competitive advantage in Canadian markets — for example, exporting, co-production agreements, and technology licensing. A cogent argument can be made that, for certain activities, direct investment and arm's-length transfers of foreign resources are imperfect substitutes. To that extent a "tax" on incoming direct investment will produce positive revenues. However, it should be noted that not all forms of direct investment are reviewable. Hence it is conceivable that, with modest changes in required outlays, internal expansion in non-reviewable forms of investment could be substituted for reviewable acquisitions. Furthermore, the opportunity for foreigners to invest in other countries offering comparable risk-adjusted rates of return provides a substitute for Canadian acquisitions.[7] In short, foreign demand for Canadian acquisitions might be highly elastic, thereby minimizing the expected proceeds of a "tax" on such acquisitions.

Effects on Competition

A long-run reduction in the number of foreign acquisitions in Canada could encourage existing firms — particularly Canadian-owned firms — to undertake a greater number of anti-competitive

---

Foreign Investment Review Agency," mimeographed, York University, Toronto, 1978.

[5] The wealth loss to foreign sellers of domestic assets (associated with a lower average selling price) is presumably of no direct concern to Canada in the short run. To the extent that foreigners see the process as a form of expropriation, it could, however, further reduce the supply of incoming foreign investment in the long run.

[6] Note that the foregone "spillover" benefits from reductions in foreign acquisitions are largely associated with reduced numbers of acquisitions of domestically owned firms, assuming that "spillover" benefits are unaffected by changes in foreign ownership of domestic assets.

[7] In this regard, it is relevant to note that income as a percentage of book value of U.S. investment was lower in Canada than, for example, in Western Europe over most of the 1960s (see I. A. Litvak and C. Maule, "The Issues of Foreign Direct Investment," in I. A. Litvak and C. Maule, eds., *Foreign Investment: The Experience of Host Countries* [New York: Praeger, 1976]).

mergers because of their increased protection against new foreign competition. Since the potential benefits of monopolization through merging depend, in part, upon barriers to new-firm entry into an industry, restrictions imposed upon the entry of foreign firms into domestic markets would increase the potential profitability of anti-competitive mergers, other things being constant.[8] To the extent that acquisitions of smaller companies facilitate "toehold" expansions by foreign firms into domestic industries, foreign acquisitions offer a uniquely important means for introducing competitive discipline into concentrated markets. The indirect consequences for competition of reduced foreign direct investment are potentially one of the most significant adverse consequences of FIRA's review process.[9]

Other Indirect Effects

Several other potentially important indirect effects of the review process should also be noted. It has been argued that foreign direct investment imposes indirect costs upon the Canadian economy by increasing borrowing costs on all other forms of foreign investment. Furthermore, under certain conditions, foreign direct investment might worsen a host country's terms of trade.[10] These two possibilities may not be particularly relevant in the Canadian case, however. Specifically, while Canada is a relatively large borrower in international capital markets, the bulk of portfolio borrowing is done by government units, whereas foreign direct investment is predominantly a source of corporate capital. While costs of capital in debt and equity markets are related, segmentation between the two markets probably exists. The likelihood that foreign direct investment adversely affects Canada's terms of trade is reduced by the observation that foreign direct investment supplies low-cost technology to Canada. Since, on balance, Canada's imports are more technology-intensive than its exports, Canada's terms of trade may actually be improved by incoming direct investment. If so, yet another indirect cost to Canada might arise from reduced foreign direct investment.

---

[8] Other forms of anti-competitive behavior, such as collusive pricing and market sharing, may also be encouraged.

[9] On the basis of his empirical work, Richard E. Caves reports that competition levels in oligopolistic Canadian industries may be higher when there is a mixture of both foreign-owned and domestically owned firms than when the industry is solely composed of one or the other. Thus, up to some limit, foreign direct investment may increase competition; however, concerns about competition from foreign acquisitions may arise beyond some "critical mass" of foreign ownership. (Richard E. Caves, "Industrial Concentration, Corporate Size and Market Power: Economic Evidence and Strategic Choices for Canadian Competition Policy," paper prepared for Competition Policy Workshop, Faculty of Law, University of Toronto, March 16, 1978.)

[10] These two possibilities comprise what have been called "first-best" arguments for restricting foreign direct investment (see H. G. Johnson, "The Efficiency and Welfare Implications of the International Corporation," in John H. Dunning, ed., *International Investment* [Middlesex: Penguin Books, 1972]).

FIRA's Effects on U.S. Incomes

It is relevant to consider FIRA's potential impact upon U.S. incomes, for several reasons. Since the bulk of foreign direct investment in Canada continues to be of U.S. origin, the impact of FIRA's review process falls heavily upon U.S. capital exporters. If the review process were seen by U.S. authorities as imposing substantial costs in terms of U.S. domestic incomes, the possibility is raised that U.S. cooperation in certain matters affecting Canada's economic welfare might be jeopardized. Moreover, any policy significantly affecting U.S. domestic income levels will have an impact upon the Canadian economy through export linkages.

In order to evaluate FIRA's potential impact on U.S. factor incomes, one must first consider the effect of U.S. direct investment abroad upon U.S. income levels. The relevant issue from the perspective of the home country is whether the social rate of return on direct investment abroad exceeds (or falls short of) that on investment at home. The argument has been made that the private rate of return on investment abroad will ordinarily exceed the social rate, since the incremental foreign investment causes wages and other factor prices to be bid up, thereby lowering rates of return earned on previous foreign investments.[11] If this effect is substantial, FIRA might promote an "improved" geographical distribution of investment on the part of U.S. firms by encouraging less investment abroad and, presumably, more investment at home.[12]

The foregoing argument is subject to a number of potential qualifications. One is that direct investment abroad might promote increased economic efficiency among firms in the home country. For example, foreign direct investment could facilitate "reverse" technology transfers from host-country to home-country firms. It could also increase economic efficiency in the home economy by providing access to foreign markets for domestic firms other than those initially investing abroad. It seems reasonable to assume, for example, that demonstrations of product reliability and service quality by individual U.S. subsidiaries redound to the benefit of all U.S. firms marketing in an area.[13] Another qualification is related to the fact that U.S. direct investment abroad may contribute to higher real incomes in recipient countries. These higher incomes, in turn, would lead to increased foreign demand for U.S. products and services, thereby promoting more favorable terms of trade for firms located in the United States. The impact of an improvement in the terms of trade is to enable U.S. residents to obtain more foreign goods for any particular level of exports.

---

[11] Put more simply, there might be a tendency for private firms to overinvest abroad.

[12] It is, of course, possible that reduced direct investment in Canada is offset by additional foreign investment in other countries.

[13] The social benefits from opening additional foreign markets to domestic suppliers derive from the existence of scale economies in many domestic industries.

Unfortunately, no evidence can be offered on the extent to which any indirect social benefits associated with direct investment abroad exceed (or fall short of) the indirect costs presumably associated with decreases in rates of return on intramarginal foreign investments. However, given the relatively small size of the Canadian market, it seems unlikely that U.S. direct investments in Canada, even if they promote increased U.S. exports, contribute significantly to realizing economies of scale in U.S.-based industries. Furthermore, technology spillovers from Canada to the United States are bound to be exceptional cases, given Canada's technological disadvantage in most secondary manufacturing industries. It is also unlikely that increased sales to Canada would effect any significant change in the overall U.S. terms of trade. Thus it is difficult to conclude on *a priori* grounds that U.S. foreign direct investment in Canada provides "spillover" benefits to U.S. factors of production. On the contrary, some evidence suggests that the after-tax rates of return on domestic (that is, U.S.) capital investments have exceeded those on U.S. direct investments in Canada when the latter are adjusted for exchange-rate changes.[14]

While the evidence is somewhat imprecise, a judicious interpretation of that evidence suggests that FIRA-induced decreases in U.S. direct investment in Canada may not have a significant impact upon U.S. domestic factor incomes. Nonetheless, one should not conclude that restrictions on U.S. direct investment in Canada will have immaterial consequences for the home country. Indeed, as leader of the free-world economies, the United States might derive important political benefits from the foreign direct investment undertaken by U.S. firms.[15] For example, the increased international mobility associated with the activities of multinational companies provides foreign-born business and labor leaders with a greater knowledge and, possibly, a greater appreciation of U.S. political and economic objectives. Likewise, the experience of and knowledge about foreign political and social structures gained by U.S. personnel working abroad provide an important source of information for U.S. policy-making in the area of international relations. Examples from Chile and elsewhere, however, can be cited as attesting to the possibility of U.S. direct investment's constituting a source of political conflict.

Summary

This abbreviated consideration of the potential direct and indirect effects of FIRA suggests that, at a minimum, the potential effects are far more complex than has to date been acknowledged in policy analyses. Furthermore, there are plausible grounds for arguing that

---

[14]See Herbert Grubel, "Taxation and the Rates of Return from Some U.S. Asset Holdings Abroad, 1960-69," *Journal of Political Economy* 82, No. 3 (May-June, 1974).

[15]A fuller discussion of such political benefits and costs is provided in the companion study contained in this volume.

the screening process, while intended to increase the net benefits of foreign direct investment, might actually impose long-run wealth losses upon Canadians. It should be stressed that such wealth losses could ensue, even if FIRA does manage to prevent specific anti-competitive foreign acquisitions and/or to capture some "rent" associated with certain foreign takeovers, if a sufficient number of acquisitions having "spillover" economic benefits were discouraged by the review process.[16]

Potential Redistribution Effects

While reductions in foreign direct investment may be presumed to impose income losses upon Canadians generally, certain specific groups in the Canadian economy may gain, at least in relative terms, from FIRA's demands upon foreign acquirers to undertake specific commitments. In the short run, the beneficiaries are those specific factors of production for which FIRA's review procedure stimulates demand increases. Several observers of the review process suggest that increased Canadian participation in management (as well as in ownership, in some cases) is one concession that is bargained for actively. Increased employment also appears to receive a strong weighting in FIRA's evaluation of an investment proposal.[17]

The determination of which specific factors of production benefit in the long run from any decreased foreign direct investment has an analogue in the income-distribution effects of a domestic tariff.[18] While the question of who gains and who loses from a tariff is quite complex, the broad conclusion is that the beneficiary of a tariff over the long term is the scarce factor of production in the country imposing the tariff. While data are admittedly incomplete and somewhat ambiguous, this author has argued elsewhere that managers and certain skilled professionals constitute the scarce factor of production in Canada.[19] In this regard, it is at least suggestive that the additional control acquired by local subsidiaries through negotiations between FIRA and parent companies has been highly praised by Canadian managers.[20] To the extent that decreased economic

---

[16]The costs associated with the operation of FIRA itself that are imposed upon the Canadian taxpayer should not be ignored.

[17]See Calvet, op. cit., p. 14, and J. Burns, "Investment in Canada: The Foreign Investment Review Act Today," paper presented at a seminar on mergers and acquisitions, York University, Toronto, January 10, 1978.

[18]The major initial contribution to this subject was made in Wolfgang Stolper and Paul Samuelson, "Protection and Real Wages," *Review of Economic Studies* 9 (1941): 58-73.

[19]See D. J. Daly and S. Globerman, *Tariff and Science Policies: Applications of a Model of Nationalism*, Ontario Economic Council Research Study Number 4 (Toronto: University of Toronto Press, 1976).

[20]Calvet, op. cit., p. 18. Calvet also suggests that the review process might increase the wealth and power of Canada's business "elite." This possibility is enhanced by the likelihood that imperfect capital mobility among domestic industries will confer

efficiency can be likened to an excise tax, the costs of reduced foreign direct investment will be regressively distributed. Thus the income-redistribution effects of the review process are potentially quite adverse.

---

long-run economic benefits upon domestic owners of capital assets in industries where foreign firms pose the greatest threat.

5

Evidence Regarding FIRA's Effects
on Foreign Acquisitions

The question of whether the long-run foreign demand for Canadian assets is altered by the review process is critical to any evaluation of the nature and magnitude of FIRA's economic effects. It is sometimes argued that FIRA's high acceptance rate for reviewable cases is evidence that FIRA is not making significant demands upon foreign investors or that foreigners have figured their way around the review process. It should be noted, however, that a high acceptance rate is also consistent with the notion that FIRA's conditions have, indeed, reduced foreign demand for domestic assets and, concomitantly, lowered the average acquisition price for domestic assets, so that the average price paid post-FIRA equals the average price paid pre-FIRA minus the monetary equivalent of "average" costs imposed by the review process on foreign investors. In effect, reduced foreign demand for Canadian assets, by leading to lower average prices for these assets, discounts the monetary value of the required commitments (and other costs to the foreign investor) in the prices paid for the smaller number of acquisitions undertaken.

A central empirical question that emerges, therefore, is how many acquisitions were foregone because of the existence of the review process. Available evidence is quite inconclusive. For example, some observers point to the fact that the annual rate of foreign direct investment in Canada declined from $725 million in 1974 to $670 million in 1975 and to –$295 million in 1976 as evidence of a worsening in the investment climate in Canada. FIRA officials argue, on the other hand, that the data on foreign direct investment have been distorted in recent years by a number of large "nonrecurring" or "irregular" transactions. These transactions involved the purchase by Canadians of some assets of foreign-owned firms in Canada and were initiated by Canadians rather than by investors wanting to withdraw capital from Canada — for example, the Canadian government's purchase of De Havilland Aircraft and Canadair Limited, the Canada Development Corporation's purchase in 1975 of most of the Canadian oil and gas interests of Tenneco Inc., and Petro-Canada's purchase in 1976 of the Alberta assets of Atlantic

Richfield.[1] FIRA officials also point out that, while the number of reviewable acquisition applications received in fiscal year 1975/76 dropped to 144 from 150 in the preceding year, the number increased to 186 in fiscal year 1976/77.[2]

The evidence cited above is inconclusive because, among other reasons, it does not explicitly control for influences on foreign acquisition behavior other than the implementation of the Act. A more explicit test of FIRA's impact upon foreign acquisitions of domestic businesses was attempted by incorporating the influence of the Act in a multiple-regression statistical model. Specifically, a number of independent variables were employed to "standardize" for other important influences upon the foreign acquisition process. The influence of FIRA was incorporated into the model by the use of a dummy variable that separated the entire sample into pre-FIRA and post-FIRA observations.[3] The analysis revealed that, holding all other factors constant, a decrease in foreign acquisitions was coincident with the passage of the Act. Furthermore, the decrease in foreign acquisition demand was of a "once-and-for-all" variety — that is, it was approximately constant over the period 1973-76. This observation belies the notion that the costs imposed by the review process upon foreigners were derived purely from inexperience with, and unrealistic fears of, the review process.

The decrease in foreign acquisitions in the early post-FIRA period might have been the result of a general deterioration in Canada's economic and political climate during the period that was not accounted for adequately by the "standardizing" variables employed in the model. Furthermore, it is possible to argue that a more detailed analysis would reveal that only certain types of acquisitions have been affected by the review process and, therefore, that a statistical evaluation of FIRA's impact upon foreign acquisitions taken as a whole might be somewhat misleading.[4] Finally, the number of post-FIRA observations was limited to those in a three-year period. Statistical inferences relying upon such a limited sample are necessarily tenuous.

These disclaimers notwithstanding, the statistical results at least call into question the notion that the review process can capture "rents" associated with foreign acquisitions without discouraging

[1] See Gilles Gratton and Marcel Custeau, "Changing Patterns of Foreign Investment in Canada," Foreign Investment Review 1, No. 2 (Winter, 1977/78): 19.

[2] See FIRA, Foreign Investment Review Act Annual Report, 1976/77 (Ottawa, 1977).

[3] A full description of this model and of the statistical results is provided in Steven Globerman, "An Economic Analysis of the Foreign Investment Review Agency," mimeographed, York University, Toronto, 1978.

[4] Calvet argues that "rents" may be present in certain acquisition categories but not in others. Therefore, the review process might discourage acquisitions in the latter category (Louis A. Calvet, Canadian Controls of Foreign Business Entry: Present Form and Future Prospects, Working Paper 959-77 [Cambridge, Mass.: Alfred P. Sloan School of Management, Massachusetts Institute of Technology, 1977], p. 21).

foreign acquisitions from taking place. Whether this failure results primarily because such "rents" ordinarily do not exist or because the review process is simply too imprecise to identify and capture "rents" where they are available cannot be answered in this
study. It is plausible to conjecture that both explanations may be
relevant in the Canadian case.

Some anecdotal evidence is available to suggest that FIRA's attempts to extract higher effective purchase prices from foreign acquirers (by demanding that foreigners undertake certain costly
commitments to increase the benefits of the acquisitions) have
brought about a once-and-for-all decrease in foreign demand for
domestic assets. Most notably, early statements by provincial governments expressed concern about the potential impact of FIRA on
foreign direct investment;[5] indeed, there is some evidence that provincial government pressures in the early stages of the Act were
strong enough to reverse previous FIRA decisions to reject an application.[6] Recent statements, however, reflect some subsidence of concern. For example, Premier Davis of Ontario remarked on a recent
trip to Japan: "I don't think that FIRA now represents the inhibition
that it did two years ago.... Businessmen I've talked to don't find it
a problem."[7] Statements such as that made by Premier Davis are
consistent with the notion that the effects of FIRA have now been
discounted in lower average prices paid for all domestic assets,
which results, in turn, from a decrease in foreign demand for domestic assets.

Another piece of evidence consistent with the hypothesis that
FIRA's screening process has decreased foreign demand for domestic
assets is a statement made by Hugh Russel Limited to the Royal
Commission on Corporate Concentration. The company indicated to
the Commission that it was able to buy two domestic firms at a discount below the price that would have existed prior to FIRA because
FIRA had greatly reduced the competition from foreign-owned
companies.[8]

It should be stressed, in summary, that evidence suggesting that
FIRA has reduced the long-run foreign demand for domestic assets
does not provide definitive evidence that FIRA has imposed net
long-run costs upon either the Canadian or the U.S. economies. It
was shown earlier that the potential direct and indirect effects of
FIRA are exceedingly complex and have positive and negative implications for income levels in both Canada and the United States.

---

[5] See, for example, Guy Saint-Pierre, "Quebec's Message to Ottawa: Don't Keep Out
Foreign Money," *Financial Post* (Toronto), January 10, 1975.
[6] Calvet, *op. cit.*, p. 14.
[7] *Globe and Mail* (Toronto), September 27, 1977.
[8] *Report of the Royal Commission on Corporate Concentration* (Ottawa: Supply and
Services Canada, 1978), p. 204.

However, to the extent that bilateral direct investment is a "positive-sum" game, the evidence tends to suggest that the review process reduces, rather than increases, the potential income benefits of foreign direct investment to both countries. At the very least, the foregoing discussion eliminates any reason to be sanguine about FIRA's economic effects based upon the low rejection rate for reviewed applications.

6

The Canadian Appliance Industry: A Case Study

It is extremely difficult to arrive at unambiguous conclusions regarding the net economic effects of FIRA's actual, as opposed to a theoretically "ideal," review process through the use of aggregative statistical analysis. An alternative approach is a detailed analysis of specific cases. Unfortunately, that alternative is hampered by a dearth of publicly available information. Furthermore, in-depth studies of actual FIRA cases provide no direct insight into FIRA's potential impact upon the initiation of foreign acquisitions. Nevertheless, the case-study approach allows the researcher to focus on specific aspects of the review process, which, in turn, may shed some empirical light on the likelihood of the process's improving the net economic benefits to Canada from foreign direct investment.

At least one recent case, involving White Consolidated Industries Limited's attempted takeover of Westinghouse Canada Limited's appliance division, generated sufficient public attention over a reasonably long period of time that some details concerning both the acquisition attempt and the review process are known. While an analysis of this case — or, indeed, of any other case — will not resolve the empirical issue of whether FIRA imposes net costs or net benefits upon the Canadian economy, it will underscore certain aspects of the review process that make it less, rather than more, likely that FIRA, on balance, improves the overall allocation of resources in the Canadian economy. Specifically, the case illustrates the extraordinary complexity of FIRA's task, which is to evaluate the outcome of specific corporate mergers and to compare the overall costs and benefits of alternative mergers. The complexity of the task is exacerbated by the very real political pressures placed upon FIRA, particularly in cases involving firms of substantial size. The WCI-Westinghouse case illustrates quite dramatically that the administrative costs of the review process to both the companies involved and the Canadian taxpayer may be quite high and, furthermore, that the distributional consequences of FIRA's decisions (whether intended or unintended) may be quite significant. It also reinforces a basic concern that can be raised about any merger-review process: the anticipated consequences of a merger may be quite different from the actual consequences.

It might be argued that the WCI-Westinghouse case is atypical and therefore inappropriate to consider. One possible objection is that it involved the transfer of intellectual property — the Westinghouse trademark — as well as the transfer of physical capital. Another is the observation that FIRA has generally allowed acquisitions by foreigners of foreign-owned firms in Canada.[1] While it is acknowledged that this case has certain atypical features, it is not clear that they constitute sufficient grounds for concluding that the case is unworthy of study. Other prominent cases will undoubtedly arise where important assets being transferred are intangible in nature. Furthermore, to the extent that the rejection of the WCI bid was atypical, it illustrates the potential for essentially political criteria to be applied in the review procedure. Specifically, it might be argued that the government's actions in the case were strongly influenced by the fact that Canada's largest domestically owned appliance company, GSW Ltd., had also expressed an interest in acquiring Westinghouse's appliance line. The specter of FIRA's being used to further nationalistic rather than strict efficiency objectives is far from being an atypical concern. Indeed, it lies at the heart of objections to the Act itself.

A Brief History of the Case

Before proceeding with any detailed analysis of the case, it might prove useful to review the relevant events. GSW Ltd. began discussions in early 1974 with Westinghouse Canada about the possible merger of the appliance divisions of the two companies.[2] However, at about the same time, Westinghouse Electric Corporation in Pittsburgh, which owned 76 percent of Westinghouse Canada, decided to sell its appliance division, including its Canadian subsidiary.[3] White Consolidated Industries of Cleveland came forward as the most likely acquirer. When White Consolidated Industries bought the U.S. Westinghouse appliance division, its Canadian subsidiary, WCI Ltd., approached Westinghouse Canada Ltd. with an offer to purchase the latter's appliance division.[4]

In April, 1975, it was reported that WCI Ltd. was offering Westinghouse Canada Ltd. $41.5 million for its appliance division. At

---

[1] Over the 1974-76 period, FIRA resolved ninety-seven proposed foreign takeovers of foreign-owned businesses in Canada. Of these, only six proposed acquisitions were disallowed.

[2] Westinghouse's appliance division included stoves, refrigerators and freezers, portable appliances, consumer service, and TV-stereo divisions and accounted for about $100 million in sales in 1973, or about 10 percent of the total Canadian household-appliance market (see *Financial Post* [Toronto], January 11, 1975).

[3] Westinghouse Electric's decision to sell its North American appliance division was motivated primarily by unsatisfactory sales and profit performance, not by GSW's overtures.

[4] WCI's appliance sales amounted to $66 million in 1973, or about 6.7 percent of the Canadian household-appliance market.

some point after the WCI offer, GSW put forth a counter-offer that was reputedly $15 million less than the WCI bid.[5] FIRA rejected the WCI bid, although White Consolidated Industries in the United States took over the appliance division of Westinghouse Electric Company in March, 1975. In early October, 1975, GSW Ltd. signed a letter of intent to purchase Westinghouse's appliance division, but the purchase was blocked by GSW's inability to acquire the right to use the Westinghouse brand name on its appliances. In purchasing the appliance division of the Westinghouse parent, White Consolidated Industries had apparently acquired the rights to the Westinghouse trademark in both Canada and the United States.

Subsequent to the blunting of GSW's purchase offer, WCI and Westinghouse Canada Ltd. announced that a new letter of intent for the sale of the appliance division had been signed by the companies. GSW Ltd., in turn, was notified that its existing agreement for purchase of the appliance division had been terminated, since the conditions in the agreement relating to the transfer of the Westinghouse trademark could not be met. However, in March, 1976, FIRA for the second time refused WCI permission to acquire Westinghouse's Canadian appliance plant, whereupon GSW Ltd. announced that it would reopen talks with Westinghouse. WCI, in turn, took steps to ensure that it would have use of the Westinghouse trademark, even if it could not acquire Westinghouse's Canadian appliance division assets, by applying to the federal trademark office to make WCI a registered user in Canada of the Westinghouse name.

Resolution of the GSW-WCI imbroglio over Westinghouse Canada Ltd.'s assets and trademark took a step forward with the formation of CAMCO to acquire Westinghouse's appliance business.[6] The formation of CAMCO, as well as CAMCO's acquisition of Westinghouse's appliance division, was apparently given the blessing of Industry, Trade and Commerce Minister Chrétien and exempted from review by FIRA. The exemption was highly unusual, inasmuch as FIRA had, up to that point, maintained that, if one of the partners to a joint venture is foreign-controlled, the joint venture should be considered a non-eligible person under the Act.[7]

Conflict over the Westinghouse trademark continued, with WCI announcing plans to market a new line of appliances in Canada under the White-Westinghouse brand name, while CAMCO argued

---

[5] The president of GSW Ltd. at the time has argued that GSW originally informed Westinghouse that it would match WCI's offer to pay book value plus an $8 million premium for the appliance division. This contention was repeated in a letter to the author from Ralph Barford, chairman of GSW and CAMCO. (See *Financial Post* [Toronto], August 16, 1975.)

[6] CAMCO was the outcome of a merger between the appliance divisions of GSW Ltd. and Canadian General Electric.

[7] In the letter referred to earlier, Mr. Barford informed the author that he was unaware that FIRA ever gave such advice.

that the introduction of a White-Westinghouse line of appliances would confuse the market. The controversy ostensibly ended, fully two and one-half years from commencement, when Westinghouse Electric Corporation assigned all ownership interest in the Westinghouse trademark and brand name for major appliances in Canada to WCI effective July 1, 1977. The assignment made it unnecessary for WCI to pursue applications for registered user status in the office of the registrar of trademarks. CAMCO, in turn, decided to launch the Hotpoint line in Canada. Hotpoint is the third-largest selling line of appliances in the United States and is owned by the General Electric Company. In addition, CAMCO established plans for a $2 million advertising campaign, the largest in Canadian appliance history, on behalf of the Hotpoint line.

While public information about the case is limited, there is some suggestive evidence supporting an argument that securing general economic benefits for Canada was not the overriding concern in the government's favoring the GSW Ltd. bid, since economic considerations favored WCI Ltd. Indeed, it has been suggested that FIRA and Donald Jamieson (then Minister of Industry, Trade and Commerce) recommended WCI be given approval to take over Westinghouse's appliance division. Jamieson's department was split on the question, with some department officials arguing against WCI. They believed that a GSW takeover of Westinghouse would help to Canadianize the appliance industry.[8] Jamieson took FIRA's view to Cabinet and was overruled. Insiders in Ottawa cite the case as evidence that government decisions about foreign investment in Canada are political as much as technical. In the WCI case the technical decision seemed to favor the U.S. company, while the political decision did not.[9]

The following section considers some technical evidence bearing on the question of whether there was a case, on economic-efficiency grounds, to favor the GSW bid over the WCI bid.

Efficiency Considerations

Before proceeding with further analysis, some background data on the Canadian appliance industry should be given. Table 6 provides plant-level data for the major-appliance industry in Canada. It should be noted that the industry classification used in the table encompasses a wider spectrum of products than were produced by either WCI or GSW. While the data are six years old, they provide certain illustrative insights into the market structure of the Canadian household-appliance industry. For example, while the majority of production establishments are Canadian-owned, over 75 percent of

---

[8] It should be emphasized that, while increased Canadian ownership would be considered a benefit under the Act, all other things being equal, the Act does not explicitly charge FIRA with the responsibility for trading off increased domestic ownership against economic efficiency.

[9] This suggestion is reported in *Financial Post* (Toronto), April 24, 1976.

TABLE 6

Domestic and Foreign Control of Establishments
Manufacturing Major Appliances, 1972

	Foreign-Owned	Canadian-Owned	Total
Number of establishments	12	21	33
	(36)^a	(64)	
Number of production workers	6,055	3,449	9,504
	(64)	(36)	
Value added (million dollars)	130.3	41.2	171.5
	(76)	(24)	

^{a}Figures in parentheses denote percentages.

Source: Statistics Canada, *Domestic and Foreign Control of Manufacturing Estab-lishments in Canada*, 1972 (Ottawa: Department of Industry, Trade and Commerce, 1977).

the industry's value added is produced in foreign-owned plants, which are substantially larger than Canadian-owned plants. Further-more, value added per production worker is somewhat higher in foreign subsidiaries than in domestically owned plants. The fact that labor productivity, on average, is higher in foreign-owned than in domestically owned plants suggests that marginal transfers of assets from foreign to domestic ownership will reduce labor productivity levels in the industry, other things being equal. This conclusion is reinforced by the observation that foreign-owned firms have gener-ally led in the introduction of new appliances into the Canadian market.

There is widespread acknowledgment of the fact that the appliance industry is marked by economies of scale and that the small Canadian domestic market restricts existing firms in Canada from capturing available scale economies. However, the precise mea-surement of both the sources and the magnitudes of economies of scale in the industry is extremely difficult. Potential scale economies exist in both production and marketing activities. Furthermore, economies of scale in production relate to both the overall volume of output and the extent of product specialization within a plant.

The difficulties associated with estimating production economies of scale are illustrated in Table 7 by the varying estimates of efficient plant size provided in two recent studies. The one compara-ble estimate is for refrigerators; it shows optimal-scale estimates ranging from 150,000 to 800,000 units per plant. Table 8 presents estimates of the unit-cost disadvantages of operating at less than op-timum size.[10] The cost disadvantages of operating at below optimum

[10]The optimum size, in this case, corresponds to the estimates in David Quirin, R. M. Sultan, and T. A. Wilson, *The Canadian Appliance Industry*, Vol. 1 (Toronto: Insti-tute for the Quantitative Analysis of Social and Economic Policy, University of Toronto, 1970).

TABLE 7

Estimates of Optimal Scale
(thousands)

Major Groups	Estimated Optimal Scale: Quirin et al.	Estimated Optimal Scale: Scherer et al.
Refrigerators and freezers	150	800
Washers and dryers	200	
Ranges	125	
Dishwashers	75	
Room air conditioners	45	

Sources: David Quirin, R. M. Sultan, and T. A. Wilson, *The Canadian Appliance Industry*, Vol. I (Toronto: Institute for the Quantitative Analysis of Social and Economic Policy, University of Toronto, 1970), p. 41; Frederick Scherer *et al.*, *The Economics of Multi-Plant Operations* (Cambridge, Mass.: Harvard University Press, 1975), p. 80.

TABLE 8

Long-Run Unit Costs As Percentages of Optimum at Different Output Levels

Major Groups	Optimum	75 Percent of Optimum	50 Percent of Optimum	25 Percent of Optimum
Refrigerators and freezers	100	105	113	125
Washers and dryers	100	110	119	128
Ranges	100	107	115	119
All groups combined	100	105	112	119

Source: David Quirin, R. M. Sultan, and T. A. Wilson, *op. cit.*, p. 43.

TABLE 9

Manufactures of Major Appliances, 1974

Appliance Group	Quantity Produced
Electric stoves	576,737
Electric dryers	314,800
Washing machines	333,499
Freezers	367,698
Refrigerators	519,645
Miscellaneous[a]	89,194

[a]Includes built-in ovens, gas cooking ovens, electric cooking mounts, space heaters, and furnaces.

Source: Statistics Canada, *Manufacturers of Major Appliances (Electric and Non-Electric)* (Ottawa, 1977).

size appear modest in light of presumed economies of scale, although it should be noted that estimates provided in Table 8 are below those suggested by some observers.[11]

While cost disadvantages of small absolute size can, to some extent, be reduced by greater product specialization, the magnitude of product economies of scale is unclear. For example, some observers argue that serious diseconomies appear to result only when products with relatively low component commonality are mixed on the same production line, since die-stamping machines, enameling units, and other such equipment can be used for a number of major appliances.[12] Other observers provide strong support for the existence of product economies of scale in the industry on the basis that changes in model mix have a significant impact upon unit costs of production for clothes dryers, refrigerators, and electric ranges.[13] Scherer suggests that product-specific economies are more important than plant-specific economies in the refrigerator industry. In short, substantial disagreement can be seen to exist on the precise magnitude of plant– and product-scale economies in the industry.

It is also of interest to consider what differential scale effects might have been expected to arise from a WCI Ltd. or a GSW Ltd. takeover of Westinghouse's appliance division. Table 9 reports total domestic production of major appliances in Canada for 1974. Unfortunately, information regarding the number of appliance units (of different types) produced by various companies is unavailable. From newspaper reports and company annual reports, one can determine that Westinghouse Canada's appliance sales were around $134 million in 1974, or about 10 percent of the total Canadian appliance market. GSW Ltd.'s appliance sales in the same year were estimated as $84.7 million, while WCI's appliance sales were estimated to be around $82 million. Assuming that GSW and WCI had roughly similar product mixes in 1974,[14] it is evident that no substantially different scale effects could have been anticipated from a WCI versus a GSW acquisition of Westinghouse's appliance division, since both companies were producing at roughly similar output rates. However, it is relevant to note that, prior to its acquisition bid, WCI had supplied Westinghouse Canada with parts. Thus some cost savings associated with a commonality of production processes would have been provided by a WCI, as opposed to a GSW, acquisition of Westinghouse.

---

[11] For example, see Frederick Scherer et al., The Economics of Multi-Plant Operations (Cambridge, Mass.: Harvard University Press, 1975).

[12] See Quirin, Sultan, and Wilson, op. cit.

[13] Harold Crockell, "The Role of Product Innovation in Trade Flows," mimeographed, School of Business Administration, University of Western Ontario, London, 1970.

[14] There is some evidence that the product lines produced by the two companies were quite similar (see Peter McDonald, "The Canadian Appliance Industry, with Particular Emphasis on the CAMCO Joint Venture," POEN 641 Research Report, York University, 1977).

It has been noted by all observers of the industry that marketing is a more important dimension of business strategy than production and that marketing economies of scale exist for multi-product firms. There is no direct evidence to suggest that GSW could have integrated the Westinghouse brand into its overall marketing activities more efficiently than WCI. Indeed, indirect evidence supports the notion that WCI's management was generally superior to that of GSW. More specifically, over the period 1972-76, net income over total assets averaged 10.1 percent for WCI and 5.4 percent for GSW. Furthermore, WCI's profit rates were also more stable than GSW's. While no direct evidence on rates of new-product introduction by the two companies is available, it was noted earlier that U.S. subsidiaries, rather than domestically owned firms, generally led in the introduction of new appliances into the domestic market. Consistently higher and more stable profit rates and faster introduction of new products support a claim for, but do not prove conclusively, superior management on the part of WCI.

In summary, while it is difficult to arrive at unequivocal conclusions regarding the relative efficiency effects of a WCI versus a GSW takeover of Westinghouse's appliance division, the balance of publicly available information suggests that some efficiency gains may have been foregone by the decision to disallow the WCI takeover.

To some extent, the subsequent formation of CAMCO is irrelevant to the basic concerns raised about the WCI takeover review process, since it might be concluded that, if the CGE-GSW merger and subsequent takeover of Westinghouse provided efficiency gains to the industry, a CGE-WCI-Westinghouse venture would have provided even greater benefits. However, it is highly unlikely that such a series of acquisitions would have received government approval. In any case, the formation of CAMCO and the government's implicit approval of CAMCO's acquisition of Westinghouse's appliance division illustrate the difficulties involved in forecasting the actual outcome of a merger.

The formation of CAMCO was seen as providing substantial efficiency gains to the Canadian appliance industry. It should be noted, however, that CAMCO has not indicated that there will be any merging of its various appliance-production facilities. Furthermore, it not only plans to continue manufacturing its existing brands (CGE, Moffat, McClary, and Beatty) but has also added the Hotpoint line. CAMCO has indicated that it will dedicate its various plants to single-product production; however, in this regard there is some evidence that, while there are advantages in having separate assembly lines for each basic appliance type, it is largely irrelevant whether this is achieved in a single plant or in separate buildings.[15] Thus there is at least some question as to whether the formation of

---

[15] See Quirin, Sultan, and Wilson, *op. cit.*, p. 9.

Canada's appliance "giant" will actually produce substantial efficiency gains.

A question might also be raised about the competitive consequences of CAMCO's formation and its acquisition of Westinghouse. These events left CAMCO with an estimated 40 percent share of the entire Canadian appliance market in 1976.[16] Competition in the domestic appliance industry has been induced largely by the leverage exerted on producers by large retail buyers.[17] The formation of a clearly dominant producer firm, which also has the potential to integrate forward into retailing, creates a significant countervailing competitive force on the supply side of the industry. Furthermore, while imports of appliances into Canada have increased recently, the substantial decline in the price of the Canadian dollar raises the prospect that domestic appliance producers may be largely shielded from foreign competition over the foreseeable future. In short, it is quite possible that any efficiency gains attendant upon the formation of CAMCO may not be passed on to domestic consumers in any case.

---

[16]This estimate is provided in *Financial Post* (Toronto), November 20, 1976.
[17]On this point, see Quirin, Sultan, and Wilson, *op. cit.*

7

Summary and Conclusions

While the case study presented in Chapter 6 is far from definitive, it tends to support concerns about FIRA raised in earlier chap-
ters. It is extremely difficult for FIRA to identify in any precise way
the expected net benefits associated with a foreign acquisition. This
difficulty is aggravated by the review process's being subject to political pressures and by the fact that the actual outcome of a merger
often differs from the expected outcome. Furthermore, the direct
costs of the review process, both to the applicant and to the Canadian taxpayer, can be quite substantial. The implication of the foregoing observations is that FIRA might discourage, albeit uninten-
tionally, a significant number of foreign acquisitions of domestic assets — acquisitions that might, on balance, have net economic
benefits for the Canadian economy.

The case also underscores a concern that FIRA's decisions may
produce significant consequences in terms of income distribution
that should not be ignored. Specifically, the president of Westinghouse Canada argued that GSW's original offer was $15 million
less than the WCI offer. Although the president of GSW Ltd. indicated a willingness to match WCI's offer, the continued support of a
group of Canadian minority shareholders of Westinghouse for the
WCI bid suggests that the WCI bid was, indeed, more favorable.[1]
Since the majority stockholder in Westinghouse Canada was a
foreigner (Westinghouse Electric Corporation), prohibition of WCI's
acquisition of Westinghouse, if its bid was indeed more favorable
than GSW's, produced a transfer of wealth from foreigners to Canadians. However, to the extent that the subsequent restructuring of
the industry involves foregone efficiency benefits, or explicit reductions in domestic levels of competition, in the appliance industry, a
continuing income transfer from domestic consumers to domestic
appliance producers (both foreign-owned and domestically owned)
will take place. The latter set of transfers is likely to be highly
income-regressive.

---

[1] The efforts of Westinghouse's minority shareholders on behalf of the WCI bid are
reported in *Financial Post* (Toronto), March 13, 1976.

It is not our contention that this monograph provides a definitive empirical evaluation of FIRA's review process; however, if the conceptual and empirical analysis presented has some credibility, a firmer basis for skepticism about the net economic benefits of FIRA has been established. At the least, a case would appear to exist for undertaking a comprehensive evaluation of the review process. Such an evaluation should involve placing heretofore confidential information at the disposal of conscientious researchers. A close scrutiny of actual cases handled by FIRA might provide further insight into whether "rent" ordinarily exists when foreigners purchase domestic assets. Analyses of the specific demands imposed by FIRA on classes of foreign acquirers, in conjunction with data on international capital flows, might also provide important insights into the question of whether FIRA, *per se*, has reduced the long-run foreign demand for domestic Canadian assets.